I0111325

How I Met God in Real Estate

REHABBED TO PERFECTION . . .
THE NEVER-ENDING PROCESS

H. TIMOTHY GRIMMETT

Copyright © 2016 H. Timothy Grimmett

ALL RIGHTS RESERVED. This book contains material protected under International and Federal Copyright Laws and Treaties. Any unauthorized reprint or use of this material is prohibited. No part of this book may be reproduced or transmitted in any form or by any means, electronic or mechanical, including photocopying, recording, or by any information storage and retrieval system without express written permission from the author/publisher.

Visit my new God-guided business, www.TimGrimmett.com, on the web and find out how to create passive income according to Christian ethics and spiritual tenets at www.AmazingLife-Now.com

ISBN: 978-1-944878-12-2

I dedicate this book to my wife, Nancy.
Without your obedience to the leading of the Lord, we would not have made it, and I would not be walking in Freedom. Thank you for not leaving me, and for loving me throughout the journey. Thank you for being patient with me through all the stages that God has taken me through in the past ten years. Most of all, thanks for believing in me in standing by my side. I do love you so much!

To the girls:
I also want to dedicate this book to my three daughters—Kayla, Jessica and Rachel—that I love so very much. Thanks for enduring this journey as a family through the ups and downs, and the tears and joys. Thanks for always believing in me as your father and allowing me to speak into your lives.

Special Thanks

Special thanks to all who helped me along the way:

Pastor Andy and Rhonda Wills, for loving me as a Christian should and taking my family in when we needed your help – at all times of the day and night.

C.P. Howard, for spiritual clarity and friendship.

Shaun McCluskey, for inviting me back into the public arena from my shame and separation.

Tamma Ford, for helping me bring this book from thought to reality.

The Holy Spirit, for pushing me to finish this work that God has given me to accomplish.

My mother, for inspiring me by telling me I could accomplish anything in life!

My father, for giving me a living example of what hard work is and what giving to others looks like.

Table of Contents

Chapter Three
Will You Listen?
Put Away Your Old Tools and Learn a New Trade

Chapter Four
Chasing Sex and Other Addictions

Chapter Five
Put Your Life in Order

Chapter Six
My Spouse Speaks

Chapter Seven
Becoming a Man-Husband-Father

Chapter Eight
Abandon Your Dreams—God's Will; Not Tim's Will

Chapter Nine
Reproduce One First, Before Many

Chapter Ten
Speak and Influence Others

Chapter Eleven
Nancy Speaks Again

Chapter Twelve
Final Thoughts

Chapter Thirteen
Lessons Learned

Introduction

Many people may wonder why I would write a book on a subject like this. Why would I be willing to reveal and discuss some of the most shameful, embarrassing, and emotionally gripping areas of my life? Why would I describe and expose my deepest failures, both personal and in business? There are four reasons I believe that I need to share this information.

First of all, the Lord put it on my heart more than ten years ago to begin writing this book, *How I Met God in Real Estate.* The first reason that I believe the book is needed is that we are in a battle—a real battle with enemies that have a desire to try to take us out. I believe the enemy tried to destroy my life through my natural weakness in the sexual aspect of my life, the weakness that progressed to a stronghold on me, to addiction, and then to bondage. It was a very real bondage in my mind. I think the enemy tried to destroy everything that I had that was valuable in my life: my marriage, my family, my business life—and my life itself. I also want to let people know that they can be set free from this bondage. There is a way that you can walk out. It's not an easy path for most, but through a system of help, prayer, fasting, and a network of people that you care and share with, there is hope.

Secondly, I want to write my story because there is simply a desperate need for this discussion in the church and in public. Men are being bound at a higher rate. We hear that almost all young men have been exposed to pornography and challenged with it. Half of the women that sit in church have been exposed to pornography and the challenges of it. It's a discussion that we need to have. It's become neglected, even taboo, and has not been talked about for so long. I have shared my story of shame with men at times, and I never thought that so many other people would relate. But often, once I've shared, they begin to tell me their struggles with the same situation. Many men are struggling with the bondage of lust and pornography, masturbation, adultery, and other perversions and strongholds on them by the enemy. I think it's time that we begin to have the conversation and begin to share with one another where there are opportunities to become free of this.

It seems as if America has created a golden idol of lust and sex; it must sell everything through sex and lusting. You can see it from commercials on TV. If you turn your sound off and watch TV, you would not have any idea what the commercial was about other than that it's selling sex and, then at the last moment, they might throw out their brand name or show their product. All of America has been changed and converted by this new god we call sex. Many people in the church were once prayer warriors, and these warriors have become weak and ineffective prisoners of war. They no longer have the power inside them to defeat the enemy because they're walking in shame. It's time that our stories changed and we began to live for God, for our families, for our wives, and those that we value.

Third, I believe that we are designed to have a relationship with the Lord and that He has designed a glorious relationship for us. That short-term lust we have substituted for love is not the correct picture that He has for us. He wants to show us His true and perfect love as in 1 John 4:18:

⁸ There is no fear in love. But perfect love drives out fear, because fear has to do with punishment. The one who fears is not made perfect in love.

He tells us that perfect love eliminates all the fear that we could experience. He will show us this perfect love, and in His perfect love, we will have no fear because we understand who He is in our life. God designed us to be in relationships. First of all, in relationship with Him, and secondly, in relationship with those people that we come in contact with, normally our neighbors and family. He says we are to love Him with our all our heart, mind, soul, and strength, and then we're to love our neighbor accordingly.

Fourth, I want to say that there is hope and abundance and joy if we truly surrender our life and live according to His plan. He said that He had glorious plans for us, that He had plans designed for us long before He even created the world, and that those plans were good and will benefit us. I have found out time and time again that the Lord's plans are better than my plans! However, you have to take a long-term view for God's plans; it's not a short-term fix like Satan tries to sell us. Satan sells the quick fix, the one that doesn't last, the one that has holes in it. If we are in tune with our Lord Jesus Christ and His Word, and follow His directives and let Him chart the path for us, there we will find victory.

I will share with you some of the stories later in the book of how I came to be imprisoned by the evil one, and how that led to my bondage. I'm not sharing this to break down anyone in my family. I'm not saying this to name names or lay blame. In fact, in those parts where using someone's name could harm him/her, I have changed the name (as they say, "to protect the innocent"), except when that individual has authored a book or program that I talk about. This book is about helping other people find freedom, not about pointing fingers or accusing anybody of anything.

Many Lessons; Many Seasons of Growth

This is not a chronological retelling of the last ten years of my life. It is about the most impactful lessons that I learned during those years as God transformed the willing vessel that I became into a new way of life. It is about how I finally accepted a new master of my life.

I had tried things my way and failed miserably. I was reckless and mired in sin and selfish ambition. I was trapped and had nowhere else to turn but God. I could not help myself. Only God had the proper tools to rehab me to perfection. I had to stay in the fire long enough to be purified, stay on the potter's wheel long enough to be shaped, and stand and endure the pruning to make me grow and produce more fruit.

I rehab homes. Buy them, fix them, sell them. It takes a few weeks to turn one house around.

God rehabs people. My true adult life—my awakened life—really started when I realized I had to surrender to God, to let Him fix me up and put me back out in the world to do His work. It took years for God to transform me.

My dad was a farmer, and sort of had that "free flow work time" going on. He worked long hours and he worked hard. And I saw that. Since college graduation, I always had some business activity going on. I started with multilevel marketing, and later, went into real estate. And like my dad, I worked long hours. However, as I later came to realize, I wasn't coming from the same mindset as he was.

While I was trying this and that to discover which business would help me make the "big time," my wife Nancy was working in the same field, having acquired her Master's in social work from the University of Missouri—Mizzou. Except for the first few years of our marriage, Nancy has been the breadwinner for our family, and consistently held one job (unlike me).

Right out of college, I started out with a salaried position for a couple of years as a District Supervisor for ALDI Foods. I then did multilevel marketing (MLM) back to back with several companies. Nancy decided to forgo working with me in multilevel marketing when we had our children. She left it to me. She had enough with her own job, the girls, and the household. I had seen us as a team, and that hurt me.

Could I explain why or how that upset me so much? Not very well. But for whatever reason, I was devastated. Maybe it was because I saw us as "Tim and Nancy"—Tim *and* Nancy, not just … Tim. We were like Batman and Robin, the Lone Ranger and Tonto, Bonnie and Clyde.

I eventually decided that MLM wasn't my way to wealth, and I went on to work with Quiktrip for seven years. It was there that a customer motivated me to purchase my first real estate property in 1999 (by the seat of my pants). I got the real estate bug after my very first deal turned a profit of around $15,000.

And then things started getting tricky. There was rapid business growth over those four years. *Was I ready or even trained for that?* Hindsight says, "No!" resoundingly! But I was all in. I was all about real estate. And, hey, I was now a CEO!

As it turned out, the Lord had to be CEO, not me.

I not only wasn't hiring God for any positions in my companies, but I also wasn't even interviewing. I wasn't letting go of my title and my pride of being a CEO. I wasn't about to appoint anyone else to my job; I wouldn't even ask God to be my business consultant.

I encountered a living, loving God during my rapid career growth. I nearly lost my marriage and family. I lost all my material wealth. I hit rock bottom from sexual and money addictions.

These are the lessons and seasons of growth that God took me through as he redeemed my life.

CHAPTER ONE

———

Sell It All; Be Debt-Free; Then Follow Me

1 Timothy 6:17

> *Command those who are rich in this present world not to be arro-*
> *gant nor to put their hope in wealth, which is so uncertain, but to*
> *put their hope in God, who richly provides us with everything for*
> *our enjoyment.*

My real estate goal was to accumulate 50 properties, pay them off by age 45, have a passive income check of $20,000 a month, and kick back with a nice stream of income. Have a house in Saint Louis, maybe a house in Colorado. Ski the slopes. Enjoy the good life.

I was working toward that. Hard. Then in 2005, the Lord stepped in and said, "I'm your security, not the bank. Sell all your properties, Tim. Get debt-free—and teach others to do the same."

Huh? Nuh-uh. I was putting my future into the real estate I was accumulating today. I was putting my hope in wealth, not in God's statement that came out of the blue.

Sell It All!

Oh, boy. Sell it all? The Lord said to—what? Every time I thought about those words of the Lord, I shuddered.

At first, I pretended that message must have been intended for someone else. For about three weeks, I refused to receive His instructions. Then, I could no longer deny that the directive was for me and that I was disobedient if I didn't sell everything. So I began the process.

Everything that I thought I was, was embodied in my real estate success—the buying and selling, the rehabbing, the profits I made. Everything I thought I was, was tied up in my real estate holdings, my businesses, my long work weeks, my reputation, my ability to do it all, all by myself. I was on track to being a millionaire.

Sell it all off? You have to be kidding!

But, by 2006, I had to buy out my business partner for $88,000. So, yes, I had debt. Three years prior, I was just $4,000 away from being debt-free in business and just blew past that into creating more debt.

Sell all my rentals—all 23 of them? Sell all my businesses and my DBAs? Let my 20-plus employees go? No way! I definitely attached my pride to my businesses and my "become a millionaire by 45" goals. How could I just drop it all? My ego stuck to real estate like white on rice. And—everyone knows—you naturally have debt when you are in business. My debt was to the tune of almost $3 million, so my debt was a huge part of my dilemma.

Rich Young Man; Money or God

It sounded like I was being told to choose God over money. I had never thought that they were mutually exclusive. Maybe they weren't for people who didn't have my story. But based on the Word that came down to me, I hunted in the Holy Scriptures for more guidance. I was sad like the wealthy man in the following parable; I can honestly tell you that was true!

Matthew 19:16–30

16 Just then a man came up to Jesus and asked, "Teacher, what good thing must I do to get eternal life?"

17 "Why do you ask me about what is good?" Jesus replied. "There is only One who is good. If you want to enter life, keep the commandments."

18 "Which ones?" he inquired. Jesus replied, "You shall not murder, you shall not commit adultery, you shall not steal, you shall not give false testimony,

19 honor your father and mother,' and 'love your neighbor as yourself.'"

20 "All these I have kept," the young man said. "What do I still lack?"

21 Jesus answered, "If you want to be perfect, go, sell your possessions and give to the poor, and you will have treasure in heaven. Then come, follow me."

22 When the young man heard this, he went away sad, because he had great wealth.

23 Then Jesus said to his disciples, "Truly I tell you, it is hard for someone who is rich to enter the kingdom of heaven.

24 Again I tell you, it is easier for a camel to go through the eye of a needle than for someone who is rich to enter the kingdom of God."

25 When the disciples heard this, they were greatly astonished and asked, "Who then can be saved?"

26 Jesus looked at them and said, "With man this is impossible, but with God all things are possible."

27 Peter answered him, "We have left everything to follow you! What then will there be for us?"

28 Jesus said to them, "Truly I tell you, at the renewal of all things, when the Son of Man sits on his glorious throne, you who have followed me will also sit on twelve thrones, judging the twelve tribes of Israel.

29 And everyone who has left houses or brothers or sisters or father or mother or wife or children or fields for my sake will receive a hundred times as much and will inherit eternal life.

30 But many who are first will be last, and many who are last will be first.

In this version of the parable, Jesus was calling his disciples and converts to "give up that material world and their pursuit of stuff and follow Him." The wealthy man parable has lots to unpack; he was sad and unwilling to sell all he had or to give to the poor.

It took me years, but I finally understood that it is our focus that changes when we transfer wealth (stuff) from one kingdom (our physical, material world) to another Kingdom (our inner world of quiet hearing of the Lord), and then we follow God's voice and obey His commands.

The transfer is to a God-focus from a worldly-riches focus. Our inner-being is much richer than our outer being could ever make us. That was a hard message for me to absorb.

We need to have a Kingdom focus. We must be willing to give up our most valued worldly possessions for Christ. We put Him in the first position.

"It is hard for someone who is rich to enter the Kingdom of Heaven."

"Rich to enter heaven" is a huge misconception. In the beginning, for me, the idea that there was no rich man in heaven was just bad teaching. That had to be all wrong. I protested it. I resisted it. I was taking care of myself, taking care of business on earth, which was where I imagined all wealth to be.

Where it talks about the camel going through the needle, I always thought it was a small hand-held needle. Once again, I thought there have to be rich people in heaven, but how do you get a camel through a needle? I did not understand that, so I reasoned that God must frown on rich people.

I was wrong with the understanding that I had of the Lord's advice. The eye of the needle happens to be a door within a door to the city. When I looked at the Scriptures from that perspective, it made sense. Walls surrounded cities in ancient times. Back then, the camel would have to get down on its knees, and they would open the low door. It prevented the city dwellers from unknowingly allowing their enemies to overtake them because only one person could get in at a time. No stampeding army could get in and suddenly overrun them. It was a protective device for the city.

The camel could fit through the door if it had nothing on its back and got down on its knees.

When I finally understood this representation, it was huge for me—and scary. This meant that a person had to get on their knees. A person had to humble himself before God. No bags of gold or treasure on our back. No house (or in my case, houses) dragging behind us. No material goods in the wagon we were pulling (or the extra-long moving van following behind us). No material concerns. No slavery to the things of the world, like concern over others' judgment of us or for keeping up materially with the neighbors.

Just us, not of the world, but in it, with a quiet faith that we are always provided for. Just us, with our heart and spirit, connected with the Lord, and the Lord guiding us. The heart within. The spirit within. The guidance from above. Just us, as who and what we really ever are. God is elevated above any and every possession we could ever own.

"Who, then, can be saved?" The scripture says that only with God's help—listening with inner-being, that heart and spirit within us—can we be saved. God saves anyone who hears Him and follows His direction and acknowledges that He is the Savior and repents of his shortcomings (sins).

Peter answered him, "We have left everything to follow you! What, then, will there be for us?" This cry of Peter's was similar to mine, and the Lord's response to me was to sell everything and relinquish my worldly possessions. I must be willing to give up all that I have in order to get all that I could never amass. An open-handed exchange. My life for Christ's life in me.

Sell It All?

After three years of real estate activity, I incorporated as Rhino Homes, which I started in the year 2000. My real estate businesses would go from about $80,000 in gross revenues to earning over $2.3 million and employing over 20 employees. I also paid large overheads (around $20-30,000/month). Within a short time, I developed eight real estate-related companies, offering all the real estate services under one umbrella: mortgage, renovation, property management, brokerage, and so forth. We would typically sell turnkey rentals to investors in California and locally to homeowners.

As for my wealth goal, I wanted to have 50 rental properties paid off by age 45 and have $20,000 a month coming in. I was relentless in pursuing that goal. I intended to live the high life, retire early, travel the countryside with my wife, and own multiple houses. The last verse of the parable talks about a reward if we follow the Lord with a spiritual mindset and openness to his blessings.

We have a Heavenly set of eternal blessings given to us by the Lord from His Kingdom. Likewise, we operate on a physical world level with its own set of blessings. The benefits show up for us differently as they come to us from two different locations. We have heavenly rewards; we receive earthly blessings. Two different worlds co-exist—the Kingdom that operates within us and the physical world that operates around us. We listen to a Christ-like consciousness in prayer, and we heed the words of the Lord. We walk our faith and trust in the Lord in our physical lives. God allows us to experience earthly blessings during this life in the physical, but He promises us that He is storing a greater treasure in heaven for us when He brings us home to enjoy life forever in His presence.

Be Debt Free and Teach Others to Do the Same

Proverbs 22:7

Just as the rich rule the poor, so the borrower is servant to the lender.

I was supposed to become personally debt-free and have debt-free businesses. That was the Lord's word to me. What is more, I was to teach others how to do the same. Hmmm, and how do I do any of that? That was my main question back in those days, for it seemed to me that I was the poster child for massive debt.

To respect the Lord's message meant I could no longer get any loans for real estate. Luckily it wasn't a problem because in 2005 I was only selling properties, not purchasing new ones. It became a bigger problem later on (I did slip up two or three times, but that is another story), and I had to learn—as the Lord was guiding me—how to make money without borrowing and to do business without any indebtedness.

Romans 13:8

Let no debt remain outstanding, except the continuing debt to love one another, for whoever loves others has fulfilled the law.

The only allowable debt was love, according to God. I found it funny because I was $2.8 million in debt. Oh, on paper, it certainly looked as if I was a cash millionaire—if I were to sell all my properties at retail prices, that is! But in reality, it was debt. A mountain of liability. It was the first quarter of 2005, the markets hadn't yet crashed, and I had just started selling off my properties.

I told my wife this liquidation would not take very long. It should only take a couple of months, and we'd be all done, debt-free, and we'd be millionaires.

Obviously, she laughed at that. A man should listen when his wife laughs at his "best" business ideas.

Follow Me and I Will Make You Fishers of Men

From Matthew 4:19

And he saith unto them, "Follow me, and I will make you fishers of men."

I did not totally understand what it meant to be committed to the Lord or why on earth I would ever want to go out and fish for people at that point in my life. I just knew that this was the Lord's directive to me.

I didn't yet know that preaching, teaching, being in my faith, or walking my spiritual talk, so to speak, was where I was being led. I didn't have any spiritual talk. Not then.

CHAPTER TWO

———

Money Is My Security, Said Tim; No, I Am, Said God

Money Is My Security

It was 2005 when I closed on a rehab deal and profited—I got a check for $111,000. It was my first check of that size. I put it in the bank. I had a real fat bank account. This was after creating eight Limited Liability real estate companies, having lots of staff, and accumulating growth several years in a row.

I did not have to balance my checking account for four to five months. Every now and then, I would roll up and check the bank account, and it'd be $80,000, $50,000, $40,000, and I just felt the excitement of not having to balance my checking account constantly.

I felt abundant, and probably more than a bit cocky about having all that cash at my fingertips.

This check came at the same time God told me to sell everything. Later, I used that cash to rehab the remaining properties so they could be sold. That is how I interpreted the Lord's message. I did not get to enjoy that fat bank balance for very long, in other words.

The Parable of the Rich Fool is what this was about. Jesus' warning is to be on guard against all kinds of greed. A man's life does not consist of having abundant possessions. And here I was, storing up that cash. I was collecting all of these "profit-generating" properties. Gobble, gobble, gobble…I was greedily collecting my wealth so that when I decided I had enough, my wife and I would just sit back and let the good times roll.

My constant thought—that I would inquire 50 rental properties and pay them off by age 45 and have net $20,000 a month coming in—was my sole business focus. In fact, it was my hard-and-fast goal and plan for myself as a business and family man. I drove it with a lust and a money-hunger. And it was my downfall. One of them…

I would kick back and enjoy life, I thought. And God said, "No. Your wealth is not in your money, but in me."

My plan was only ever about accumulating wealth for retirement. But here's the rub: there is no retirement in the Bible! Wealth accumulation really just replaced my sports drive and achievements in sports. I didn't do the competitive sports anymore, so my new challenge, my new yardstick for measuring my own success, was "how much wealth do I have?" All my focus was on generating that mountain of money!

Maybe I wasn't as well-schooled as I should've been in the realities of creating wealth and becoming a wealthy man…maybe not as schooled as I could've been about business and the business of real estate.

I bought into the American Dream—education, job, climbing the corporate ladder, planning a family, saving for retirement, etc. Or should I say American Nightmare?

I had also bought into the false belief that there is good debt and there is bad debt. Leading real estate trainers advocated "good" debt (any borrowing associated with an income-producing asset could be called good debt). Bad debt? That's a house with a mortgage on it, a car with monthly car payments on it, or family vacations you put on a credit card. It is your monthly bills, really.

So I slipped up in fully understanding the worldly rules of finance and wealth building. But I was also totally oblivious to the spiritual laws and rules for creating wealth!

I had cash in the bank, but I had to use it to rehab the remaining investment properties because I could not use debt financing anymore. I could not borrow any more money to buy more houses. No more debt. I was trying to stick with that directive.

This taught me something awful that business owners just don't want to hear—profit and cash flow. No businessperson wants to hear that his most beloved product makes a loss each and every time it is sold! I learned the hard way that I was not really making any profit on a property when I was rehabbing it. I was "rolling cash," which meant that if I was short on one property, I'd just borrow money from the next property and use it to pay off the mismanagement of the first property.

"Rolling cash forward" was not my smartest business move. I was doing the proverbial "stealing from Peter (me) to pay Paul (me)." Oh, boy.

The Parable of the Rich Fool is what this was about. And I still wasn't getting it … I was acting like the Rich Fool.

Luke 12:17–19; 20–21

> *17 And he began reasoning to himself, saying, 'What shall I do, since I have no place to store my crops?'*
>
> *18 "Then he said, 'This is what I will do: I will tear down my barns and build larger ones, and there I will store all my grain and my goods.*
>
> *19 "And I will say to my soul, "Soul, you have many goods laid up for many years to come; take your ease, eat, drink and be merry."'*

I had forgotten to read the rest of the story:

[20] *"But God said to him, 'You fool! This very night your life will be demanded from you. Then who will get what you have prepared for yourself?'*

[21] *"This is how it will be with whoever stores up things for themselves but is not rich toward God.*

I am going to continue to grow. Continue to grow and put everything back for me and my family to enjoy at a later date. Money in the bank makes me and my wife feel better as we are set up for any future downturns. America and Americans count on the bank and think "I've got this!" But that is a wrong mindset; our dependency and faith in God are diminished. Nancy and I have got this—with God!

I Am Your Security

God essentially said, "I am your security in the world," and I thought I had to store up enough on my own to have my security locked in. That I could provide for myself and my family if I salted enough away.

I have never relied on anyone, certainly not on the Lord, in a real, trusting way. Not during all those past years. I look back and I know where that belief—that I'm on my own to "make it" and I'm on my own "when trouble comes"—started. It is difficult to deal with beliefs or lessons that we hold as truths. We learned almost all of them as children, and that makes it hard to dig them out of our past.

First, the trick is to identify the lesson and find the beliefs buried in those years, deep inside our subconscious!

Second, you have to swallow your pride and fear, and your sadness too, maybe, and decide if you should allow the belief to run your life anymore.

Then, you must forgive yourself for being controlled by that false belief. After all, you were a defenseless child when you first believed, and the belief seemed to serve a purpose. Now, though? Not so much.

I found the source of my limiting beliefs. There were two big events in my young life that formed the belief, "Tim cannot rely on anyone but himself."

The first happened when I was around six years old. I went to a basketball game, and our mascot wore a bobcat outfit. That night I woke up and looked out my window. I could vividly see this bobcat standing at the window.

He was about six feet tall, and the fear chilled my blood, so I went into my parents' room and said, "Hey, I'm scared! There's a bobcat, you know, outside my window." Obviously, there wasn't, and they told me to go back to bed.

I swear, every time I opened my eyes and looked out the window, there was this bobcat. The second time I returned to their room, I insisted, saying, "There's this bobcat still standing outside my room."

However, my third visit was one too many. After they had dismissed me yet again, I stared out my bedroom window until my father surprised me by appearing in my room and giving me a spanking. The one and only spanking he ever gave me … but it let me know that I should fear my father more than that bobcat outside my window. I never bothered my parents again with my visions.

The second incident occurred not too far from that time. As I walked to school each morning, two boys tormented me incessantly. I told my father, again in vain. I told my teacher, also in vain since she never took action. And I didn't have an older brother that I could rely on to fight my battles for me. This was something that I had to face up to myself.

So I told my mom about it. Was I told by my mother that I was supposed to fight these two guys? Yes! Because the teacher never did anything, my mother told me to take it into my own hands and take care of it. And I did. When it happened, and I told my teacher what my mother had told me, the teacher phoned my mom. Mom supported my story, and I wasn't disciplined.

It happened like this. I walked about three blocks to kindergarten from my babysitter's house. One day on the way to kindergarten, I placed a stick behind the tree that they always had to pass. When they later chased me, I ran to the tree, retrieved the stick, and fought them off. I looked forward to getting into trouble later that day because my mom had told me exactly what to do when the teacher confronted me.

From then on, I pretty much believed that I couldn't depend on anyone and that if it's up to me, it was going to have to be through my power alone.

I was looking at my Heavenly Father (God) as I looked at my earthly father. That created an improper image of the true Living God for me. My earthly father was a father who believed in discipline and working for his approval. Given that belief, I wasn't looking at my Heavenly Father through the right eyes. I learned that we have to dig out and let go of old beliefs because so many of them keep us from hearing and trusting in the Lord's guidance and love.

Proverbs 3:5–6

> ⁵ *Trust in the Lord with all your heart and lean not on your own understanding;*
>
> ⁶ *in all your ways submit to him, and he will make your paths straight.*

My childhood beliefs went against God showing up when I needed Him—like a Cosmic Genie—not when He needed me or wanted to present Himself to me. The Lord told me my security was in Him. The "old way" of perceiving God trapped me with the belief that "Tim's on his own." The "new way" was to be in Christ, and to trust His way and rely on Him; to hear and follow His guidance on a daily basis. By following His commands, my life took a new direction with fewer turns, mishaps, and frustrations.

Depending on my intuition, thoughts, old beliefs, and failed attempts would never be as effective as abiding the Lord's guidance.

2 Corinthians 5:17

> *Therefore, if anyone is in Christ, the new creation has come: The old has gone, the new is here!*

Then, also in Hebrews, it talks about our faith, which is not anything that we can see or touch—it's intangible. It is in our heart and spirit within.

Hebrews 11:1–3

> *¹ Now faith is confidence in what we hope for and assurance about what we do not see.*
>
> *² This is what the ancients were commended for.*
>
> *³ By faith we understand that the universe was formed at God's command, so that what is seen was not made out of what was visible.*

So, this was the place that imprisoned me. Of course, for years and years, I didn't even think of myself as being stuck! Not at all. I was simply working and slaving away at my worldly wealth just like everyone else.

I know now that we are all the result of old childhood beliefs and stored memories, but I didn't know it then and, frankly, I didn't even care to examine any archaic beliefs as the cause of my struggles. I felt justified doing what needed to be done to achieve a goal; it's what any businessperson ever did. It never occurred to me that the Lord defined this as the "old way!" Struggle is the old way.

Even if I had known the Lord's "new way," as defined in Proverbs 10:22, it would have seemed so weird and unfeasible to me. I would've blown it off and kept on (as I did for another little while).

Proverbs 10:22

> *The blessing of the LORD brings wealth, and He adds no trouble to it.*

I struggled to accept and see God as He is; not as I see my earthly father. "Wealth without toil" made no sense to me. None. That was like wishful thinking. Things just didn't happen that way in this world of mine! The Kingdom way is very different from the worldly way of operating. We must replace old ways and belief systems with the truth of God's word.

CHAPTER THREE

—

Will You Listen? Put Away Your Old Tools and Learn a New Trade

Will You Listen?

Learning to listen to the Lord. Consciously listening for the Lord and His guidance. That was part of the 12-step Sexaholics Anonymous program I used to heal, abandoning myself to the Higher Power aspect I call God.

It's the ugliest part of my life, I believe.

I committed adultery and got caught red-handed. The woman's husband secretly tape recorded us with a device placed under the bed as we were talking on the phone together about our relationship. I suffered a sexual addiction which I didn't identify as such until my therapist called it to my attention. I just thought of it as feeding the lust within myself, the never-ending hunger, the hunger that caused me to try more and more degrading feats. A porn addiction ate away at me, too. I had to begin to break away from these compulsions, these addictions.

In this phase of my life, I frequently read the Bible. As I went through the 12-step program, I saw that the other participants utilized systems. The "going step-by-step" aspect worked for them and also for me. I had an accountability partner, a sponsor.

I read a small library of books to understand and recognize what I did as I shared my adultery and addictions with my wife. There is never a good time to create pain for someone you love. I came clean with Nancy right away, and we went to our pastor the next night. He suggested I start reading the Bible as if my life depended on it and really going deep and seeking answers to become free from my addiction.

The pastor counselled us. He said if we hoped to hold the marriage together, we'd need both a spiritual and worldly process to repair the breaches. If we asserted faith in God's ability to do the impossible, we could heal. We could hold the marriage together by welding it like two pieces of metal—stronger at the welded joint than ever before. We could give hope to others— even as we repaired our own trust and faith in each other—if they were going through a similar challenge.

Divorce wasn't on the table. Nancy intended to help me, as you will read in her own words later. My agenda involved practicing honesty and healing everything my addiction jeopardized.

My research and my will slowly educated and released me from the struggle of the last 25 years of negative behavior, basically from ages 13 to 36. Porn addiction, defiance, and repeated sexual acting-out episodes—these were all part of the same pattern of addiction. The pattern wasn't continuous, however. I would have years of reprieve, and then, out of nowhere, the darkness attacked whenever I came under intense stress or financial pressures.

It took eight months of rigorous studying and reading the Bible until one day I just noticed that, in my head, it stopped. The double-mindedness evaporated. (I'll talk about the fasting

I did, too. That was a key. A big key.) Whatever had been controlling me, it lifted off me that day. No more constant mental conversations in my head of good versus bad.

My mind had always contained two voices. I was double-minded. A second man kept telling me what I had to do, what I needed to do NOW—and I couldn't control him. I couldn't sit by myself and be still. I always had to be busy, doing something, anything. I could not stand myself when I was not actively doing something.

I feared that someone would find out who I was, even though that second man tried to convince me that it was "our little secret." Of course, part of that second man's message was, "If my wife ever found out, if she ever knew what I have been doing behind her back, she'd leave me. I'd lose the family. I'd lose the girls. Keep quiet about this other life." And I couldn't stand the thought of losing them.

But how do you diminish such a risk in the midst of uncontrolled behaviors and double-mindedness?

Double-mindedness? God turns you over to yourself. You think you know what is right, but you don't. There is a push-pull between what is right and what is wrong. Too often what is wrong is the stronger one, and you cave into it.

Galatians 5:19–25 (The Battle of Double-Minded)

19 The acts of the flesh are obvious: sexual immorality, impurity and debauchery;

20 idolatry and witchcraft; hatred, discord, jealousy, fits of rage, selfish ambition, dissensions, factions

21 and envy; drunkenness, orgies, and the like. I warn you, as I did before, that those who live like this will not inherit the kingdom of God.

22 But the fruit of the Spirit is love, joy, peace, forbearance, kindness, goodness, faithfulness,

23 gentleness and self-control. Against such things there is no law.

24 Those who belong to Christ Jesus have crucified the flesh with its passions and desires.

25 Since we live by the Spirit, let us keep in step with the Spirit.

Romans 7:21–25 The Struggle Within: Flesh versus Soul

21 I find this law at work: Although I want to do good, evil is right there with me.

22 For in my inner being I delight in God's law;

23 but I see another law at work in me, waging war against the law of my mind and making me a prisoner of the law of sin at work within me.

24 What a wretched man I am! Who will rescue me from this body that is subject to death?

25 Thanks be to God, who delivers me through Jesus Christ our Lord! So then, I myself in my mind am a slave to God's law, but in my sinful nature a slave to the law of sin.

There are certainly other scriptures (from James and other books) that speak about the double-mindedness we suffer from. The Lord knew the risks of being human. The scriptures prove this. The scriptures also state the remedies.

At the point when the hold on me lifted, I became a new person. I experienced a definite shift. I didn't care what other people thought of me. I didn't care what was in my past or who knew my past. I felt free for the first time. I could just sit by myself, content to do so for the first time. I could be quiet. I could be alone, at peace. I didn't have to be moving so fast.

It took some time to adjust. It was a while before I could share my story, the whole story. Shame and guilt still consumed me.

For the first part of my adjustment, I simply read the Scriptures. I focused on the Lord during my new morning ritual— spending an hour and a half to two hours every morning reading the Word.

The second part of this change came by learning too fast and reaping the benefits of my prayer-plus-fasting approach. I also incorporated prayer and journaling.

Fasting—The Petition

A pastor I saw on TV named Jentezen Franklin, who advocated and led 21-day fasts for his parishioners, inspired me to discover the benefits of fasting-plus-prayer for myself.

I realized that the sexual pull and cravings left my body and mind during fasting-plus-prayer periods. It gave me freedom from my sexual addiction and freedom from the pull of business and money. It gave me "access" to the Holy Spirit.

If only a man could fast forever!

I started fasting in January 2005, and I progressed from full three-day fasts to week-long fasts and then 2-week fasts. Eventually, I trained myself to do a 21-day fast with Jentezen. I've since done 21-day fasts numerous times.

Today, I sometimes initiate a fast when I need an answer or am in a dry spot—when I'm not hearing or feeling close to God. If I want to better attune myself to the quickening (the hearing, knowing, and awareness) of the Holy Spirit, I will initiate a fast.

As my fasting experience expanded, the simple purpose revolved around drawing closer to God, which eliminated temptation.

James 4:7–8

> *7 Submit yourselves, then, to God. Resist the devil, and he will flee from you.*
>
> *8 Come near to God and He will come near to you. Wash your hands, you sinners, and purify your hearts, you double-minded.*

I realized a lot about our connections to the world—not just my own but also the push-pulls that tempt all. The pull of money, in other words. Food is just another routine habit, which is just a habit of bondage, not really freedom. I saw that when I didn't eat with my family, I missed moving my mouth! We think we have a wealth of food choices in our culture, but it is a lure and a lie—just a habit. Watching commercials without sound is another enlightening experience. It's all about food or sex to sell products, and it's crazy.

We are compelled to be out in the world always doing something, but our real fear is that we'll miss out on something if we are not struggling, competing, and doing more than anyone else. It takes over you. It took over me, with my long working hours and my struggle to achieve wealth-based goals.

I just kept focused on my burdens and my process of letting them go.

I realized, too, that the fasting brought mental clarity. Sometimes we are afraid of that. The clarity and the quiet are so foreign to us in everyday living. During fasting days 11–17 for me, my body slows down and comes to a resting place. At this time, I find myself experiencing tunnel vision and tunnel listening (blocking out everything around me) and I am one with the Holy Spirit. The body no longer processes foods, and I feel rested and cleansed from inside.

Our culture tempts us into self-indulgence. I saw that gradually, too. Wanting more money and going after it? Self-indulgent. Seeing that woman and going after her in spite of commitments to the contrary? Self-indulgent. Eating certain foods because it's the weekend or it's party time? Self-indulgent. No self-control. What a trap …

I found that fasting supercharged my praying and my ability to hear the Lord from my silence— from His silence. To feel real freedom from the world, right there while I was in the world. That is quite a zone to be in!

This said, about 16 to 24 months after my initial confession to Nancy, and practicing what I began in 2005, still steeped in the Word, I noticed the burden lifting. I felt strong enough and free enough to share testimony with strangers about my addiction and this new freedom. Nancy and I had told the members of our church from the beginning. I felt moved to share beyond our congregation.

Fasting taught me how to listen to the Lord, how to hear Him, that He would speak to me through the Holy Spirit—not so much audible words but through a quickening of my spirit, guiding and providing for me.

I wanted to hear what God had for me, and I would just get alone with myself and with Him. There's a point during the fast when you go into a "zone" and you block everything else out. It is also the only time I feel totally free from the sexual compulsions and from the behaviors that come with addiction.

There was no pull on me—either on my mind or my body—whatsoever during any extended fast. After about day eight or nine, I was just totally in the zone. The Lord would speak to me, and I wrote what He gave me in a journal, along with my own thoughts.

I would hear from the Lord what my purpose was and what the Lord would use me for. These were just moments of quietness; just a time where I could commune with God. He would talk to me, and I would just write things down. It was a sweet time. I needed those moments.

Early Christians regularly fasted and prayed as a spiritual commitment up until the 5th century. We primarily sought a spiritual connection to Christ, and then we lost it as a spiritual directive, unlike the Jews and Muslims of today who continue with the annual Jewish Yom Kippur and their weekly Sabbath and with the Muslim's month of Ramadan. Why did Christians stop their fasting commitment? We don't know. All we can do is pick up the commitment again for ourselves.

About 60% of the references to fasting as a spiritual discipline reside in the Old Testament. The teachings of Scripture today in its newer versions don't emphasize fasting with prayer like the past versions do, and the Christians of today suffer this loss. Whenever I see the words "through prayer" in the Scriptures, I think "through prayer and fasting," and it makes sense to me.

This pivotal Old Testament chapter of Isaiah, which modern Jews specifically read out each year at Yom Kippur, their High

Holy Day of spiritual fasting, needs to be taken to heart by us all. Why? Fasting takes us from our body-focus, our focus on the world, into a focus on God and hearing Him clearly. Here is an excerpt:

Isaiah 58: 6–8, 11 (True Fasting)

> *⁶ Is not this the kind of fasting I have chosen: to loose the chains of injustice and untie the cords of the yoke, to set the oppressed free and break every yoke?*
>
> *⁷ Is it not to share your food with the hungry and to provide the poor wanderer with shelter—when you see the naked, to clothe them, and not to turn away from your own flesh and blood?*
>
> *⁸ Then your light will break forth like the dawn, and your healing will quickly appear; then your righteousness will go before you, and the glory of the LORD will be your rear guard. […]*
>
> *¹¹ The LORD will guide you always; He will satisfy your needs in a sun-scorched land and will strengthen your frame. You will be like a well-watered garden, like a spring whose waters never fail.*

So part of listening to God was putting my tools away. This involved no longer working alongside my real estate employees, I guess. Deciding to listen more closely to God led me to pick up new Spiritual tools like reading the Word, praying, and fasting.

Put Away Your Tools

Financing my properties, since God had told me I could have no more debt, became a mental game of avoidance and excuses at first. As I sold off my properties, I still tried to make real estate work without borrowing money. I practiced self-deception in the process, calling debt by other names or non-traditional ways of dealing with my cash flow. I just couldn't understand where the money went. It was no way to stay in business, certainly no way to run a stress-free business.

I wanted to listen to the Lord about this because then I would know where my money was—and that it was mine—all the time. Two or three times in 2011, though, I borrowed money. I slipped up on the guidance to not borrow money.

I designated one loan to rehab a house for an unmarried couple. I found that I judged the couple and even said to them point-blank, "I should charge extra because you're not married but living together." Oh, man! Here I was judging people and all the while I was not obeying the Lord's directive to me. What is that about casting the first stone? Well, the Lord "spoke" to me about that judgmental thinking, because … there was no money left in the deal for me when I closed that transaction! No profit at all! Nothing. Just a lot of work arguing with the customer, resulting in lost time and no reward.

You'd say, "Go ahead and knock your head against the wall, because you didn't listen." But no! I went ahead and repeated the same mistake two more times. I borrowed against the Lord's counsel … and didn't profit on either of those deals.

Not borrowing money means what, then? I could borrow it and lose it, or I could come out at zero at best. I could borrow and get lost in not being able to account for it, just like I'd been doing.

Who knew that God was a source of business training! It goes further, with a lesson from Him about working in the business versus on the business.

I was always one who wanted to work beside my men, with my crews. I wanted to train my guys how I wanted the projects completed. Yes, I was a control freak, but later, God taught me how to run a business. Who could ask for a better mentor?

Even though I didn't have the carpentry skills that they possessed, I wanted to be there. I brought the materials. I kept the timeline going. I did what I could do.

A comment that I always made was, "We're not living here. Just get it done good and fast." I wasn't one for the fancy house rehabs. I wanted to put it back cleanly, meet all safety and building codes so it was useful and functional, and sell it or rent it out as soon as I could.

God kept pressing me to stop working in the business, to stop second-guessing and micromanaging my crews on the sites. God pressed me to work on the business: I needed to step back and be a big-picture strategist and do things more sanely. I needed to get quiet and hear how the Lord guided me to operate my business. I forgot that by telling me "no more debt," He was indeed showing me one strategy for working on my business.

I'll say that again: stop working in the business and work on the business. Like in the E-Myth book by Michael Gerber that I read ... I was doing the $10/hour work instead of hiring that out and focusing my skill and attention on the $200/hour work. I needed to do the strategic and visionary work, not the daily tasking.

Working on the business necessitated the ability to identify the things that went wrong around the time when I experienced rapid growth. That question was a "working on the business" question. I had never duplicated myself or other key people—also a "working on it" question.

In my first full year, I did $187,000 in gross sales. The next year, I did $1,669,000 in gross sales. I had grown extremely rapidly, to say the least. I may not have had the formal real estate training but acting as if I did seemed to be working for me!

I didn't have time to put things in place like I should have so that I possessed reliable processes. I didn't duplicate myself so that I could get more done in the same amount of invested time. I didn't have the right people; I took just anybody that came along that could fill the spot with passion and enthusiasm. That was also due to how rapidly we were growing the business. We just made it up on the fly, and it worked.

There were five or six businesses in my operations. There was the construction company. There was a real estate company. There was a property management component. There was a mortgage company. There were so many companies that we exploded into that year. I did not put processes in place or any procedures to help staff. I didn't even know what to put in place because the various businesses were growing and I didn't know what I didn't know.

We were trying to figure out how to pay people and come up with fair compensation plans. It finally dawned on me that some policies and procedures would be not only helpful but necessary! Eventually, all I got around to doing was putting out fires.

My business partner handled most of the office operations. I handled most of the field operations. We did, in time, begin to put some policies and procedures in place.

The Lord took me back through those moments of craziness and fast business growth and said, "Go back and review what it was that went wrong as you grew the business, how you failed to put the business in order." The Lord acted as my business coach!

Learn a New Trade

Here is when I transformed from being a full-time real estate investor to a full-time pastor. The Lord called me into ministry as a result of 1) such deep study in the Word, 2) not running from Him any longer and 3) now listening to and for Him.

It was the J-term for Free Methodist Pastor ordination classes. I was in class with ministers from our denomination. There were two one-week classes. I fasted during the week leading up to the first class, in search of a great spiritual experience and I had one. I experienced an incredible intensity with the Holy Spirit. He just washed over me. I can only describe it as a painful but overwhelming type of real joy, with lots of tears. I didn't know whether to cry or laugh. The whole class received a spiritual experience that week in early January, as it happened.

In late 2009, I was appointed to lead a small church and did so for five years. I matured in my ministry during this time, leading this church and finding out what was required of me to lead.

I remember making this statement to a senior retired pastor: "I do not feel like I'm worthy to be used by God." He responded, "You are not worthy to be used by God."

It shocked me that he would say that. I guess I expected a boost to my ego or some kind of encouragement, but he said, "God doesn't ask us to be worthy. He only asks us to be willing." He said, "Are you willing to serve?" And I said, "Yes."

I didn't know what that meant, though. The cost of being willing to do whatever the Lord wanted to be done? How could I measure up to that?

Several years earlier, our local minister witnessed the frustration in my life and the things I attempted in the world of real estate with one business after another after another. He said, "Tim, if you're continuing to be frustrated, you probably have the call of the Lord on you. So go out and try all that you want to try and become frustrated, but if that continually happens to you, you may have a call on your life."

He was so right. He somehow foresaw where I was headed.

My wife would tell you that I've tried so many different businesses that it's ridiculous. So many new starts and so many different types of business. From selling jewelry to several network marketing businesses, to anything you can think of. I've gone through at least 20 or 30 different sets of business cards that remind me how I was trying to find out what it was that I was supposed to do with my life.

Each time coming up short. What was God's design for my life?

I realized, or I told myself anyway, that I was not smart enough to be a pastor. God said to me, "I'll teach you. Be careful about going to [seminary] school today and what you could be taught, because they may teach you the wrong ideas in a way that the common person may not be able to apply the Word to their lives. So study your Bible, get up and read. I will help you interpret and give you the revelation as to what passages mean, but you are going to have to K.I.S.S.: Keep It Super Simple. Make your ministry and scripture interpretations practical so that those you instruct will be able to live out God's commandments every day. Keep your ministry simple. Teach basics from the spirit.

Fundamental items. It's real simple. Do not get caught up in the denominational division."

The need is for our purpose to match our passion. We have so much choice today, overwhelmingly so. There are choices connected to money outcomes that don't align with our life purpose or passion—nor with our God purpose. I learned, inch by inch, to let God guide the money outcomes to me as I put my faith in Him as opposed to letting my addictive behaviors or the world of business tempt and guide me. That hadn't been working, anyway.

This is what the Lord shared with me. It is about living in the world and being Holy unto the Lord. It is about being pliable, usable, humble and willing to help the least of these with love through truth. That is probably what the pastor was getting at when he told me, "You just have to be willing."

I'm a father, with many other fathers in our congregation. With the problems our college-bound and younger children are having today—books, testing, life experiences, relationships, judgments and opinions, listening to God's lead—we parents need to assist our children more judiciously. As we walk, talk, work, and meditate on His word, we teach it to our children. We must seize those teaching situations that arise in the home, as well as do our own learning.

I need, as all parents need, to talk about the challenges as they come up in daily life with our children. With my daughters, for sure. With the younger group in our congregation, as well. This, too, is what the Lord shared with me. But K.I.S.S. with them, too.

As a senior pastor tells me, you cannot teach a concept to others before God has thoroughly taught it to you. You must live it before you can teach it.

In my journey now, I am discovering how to help people live an *AMAZING LIFE*. I like to capitalize and italicize those words! [www.amazinglife-now.com] What is it? I am in the process of learning and teaching the following:

1. Live debt free
2. Live bondage free
3. Find your purpose and passion in serving the Lord

Joshua 1:8

> *Keep this Book of the Law always on your lips; meditate on it day and night, so that you may be careful to do everything written in it. Then you will be prosperous and successful.*

Deuteronomy 11:18–21

> *[18] Fix these words of mine in your hearts and minds; tie them as symbols on your hands and bind them on your foreheads.*
>
> *[19] Teach them to your children, talking about them when you sit at home and when you walk along the road, when you lie down and when you get up.*
>
> *[20] Write them on the doorframes of your houses and on your gates,*
>
> *[21] so that your days and the days of your children may be many in the land the LORD swore to give your ancestors, as many as the days that the heavens are above the earth.*

There is a pleasant kind of joke among my daughters' friends that our house feels holy and protected because, as in verse 20 above, my family and I posted over 40 written scriptures all over the house on the walls, mirrors, doors, fridge, etc. (The book "Word Speak" has memory verse cards you can purchase. See item 6 in the Bibliography).

Three basic things became my focus in my personal life and public ministry:

1. **Love God**—Two questions I constantly asked myself were, "What does it mean to love God? Can I love Him if I am not listening to His guidance, following His Son, and being in His image with my behaviors and words?"

2. **Love People**—Help people in life; help them find salvation. Care for widows, orphans and fostered kids, the sick, and those in need. Lend a hand. Extend compassion.

3. **Make Disciples**—Questions I asked myself were, "Is anyone following me as I am following Christ? Am I

following Christ? What is the fruit in my life? To whom am I teaching God's principles?"

The Great Commandment and the Great Commission was God telling me that there's more than enough right in those two things to keep my life full even as I strive to accomplish them. I no longer had any need to get caught up in all the little things that divide the church today and set us one above the other. There's more than a lifetime of things to do just in loving Him, loving people, and making disciples. Let's not fight over the minor issues of Christianity. We can all agree on these two directives.

My Ordination Process

For six years, I studied part time to be an ordained pastor, taking classes each year.

I intended to grow my real estate business and donate or volunteer my time to the church. Let me tell you what the Lord said. "No!"

I felt stumped. No? Is He saying no church work? Or no real estate work? How do I earn a living, I wondered. God said, "You start working in the church right now, and we'll worry about the for-profit business later."

The Lord meant for me to leave my money-making businesses? What!?

But I listened. I took heart and had faith. I started out working in the church, donating my time at first and, at the same time, winding down my business activities. Not getting into any more debt with those three ridiculous exceptions I spoke about earlier, and selling the rehabbed properties already in my portfolio.

I was voted, by the congregation, to serve the church when our ordained pastor left. I was then officially appointed 11 months later by our conference superintendent.

Obviously, I didn't know how to preach. I didn't have any clue. We chose to get another pastor from the conference (an ordained college professor), and he would come in and tutor me.

I would preach two weekends out of the month, and he would preach the other two weekends until I learned how to prepare a sermon within a week and give one per week.

I took over a small family congregation, which was quite loving and dysfunctional at best. Nancy and I had been part of the congregation for 19 years. It was a group of people who, for the most part, were all country people living in the big city. I'm from the country. I'm a rural farm boy by nature. We found ourselves in the midst of a big city. We live in St. Louis, and all of us desired to be in a congregation that was close-knit, small, and intimate with one another. We shared our lives, our pain, our joys, and our struggles. We began to grow and function as a single unit over time.

It was a wonderful time of training and growing for me. I learned what it meant to hear people, grow with people, struggle with people, and laugh with people. I learned social work on the fly (Nancy is the family professional there). I learned how to just simply be there for people. All of this God poured through me and into others.

I was growing and learning and at the same time helping others do the same. I didn't know what I was doing; it was just trial and error, I went with a God given flow. It was by the grace of God that He helped me walk that path.

Be My Tool—Just Be Obedient to Me

What does it mean to be God's tool? It means you get no glory! You get to put your heart and soul out there, but not take any of the credit.

There's nothing for you. There's no praise for you. No one ever asks what tools you used to create any masterpiece you've come up with. Any time you see something, you don't walk up and say, "Oh, I wonder what tools they used to create this building, or what tools they used to create this masterpiece." No one asks that. The only thing others ask you is, "Who was the designer? Who put this together?"

I dedicated myself to a bondage-free role, available for God's use. That was my only purpose. I found it necessary to respond whenever God called me into action. I had to be addiction free. Even though I struggled with sex, money, and the lure of the next business deal, I was continuously accountable. I agreed to hold an empty bucket with Nancy, meaning I had to confess my sins to her if I had a slip-up in my sobriety and that I would empty that bucket right away and tell her my shortcomings. I had to be repentant and walk with a clear conscience. I could never give Satan grounds to highjack my thoughts.

How did I work through this time in my life? How did I clean it all up? I received help from a real estate friend who told me, "You are not that shame; it is not who and what you are. Stop using it to describe yourself and your situation." He made me come out of hiding and start telling a new story.

Shame confounded me at this point. That's what was needed, I think—real hard talk from a close friend. As God said in Romans, all things will be used. He'll use my shame like any other tool. He'll turn all this junk into a tool, because as that popular saying goes, "God don't make no junk." That's what happened to me. Satan uses shame to keep us from being useful and living for Christ. There is no condemnation in Christ.

Romans 8:28

> *And we know that in all things God works for the good of those who love him, who have been called according to his purpose.*

Romans 8:1

> *There is therefore now no condemnation to them which are in Christ Jesus, who walk not after the flesh, but after the Spirit.*

There's no way I could have pastored out of my arrogance before picking myself up from my fall. I was in no position to do so in those years. I may have acted like I had confidence in plentiful supply, but it was a lie.

I would say "confidence." My wife would say "arrogance." I truly know now that it was arrogance, even though the very word throws up my resistance to it. Humility helps me today as a pastor. I humble myself whenever I speak to a congregation member or else I cannot help him. However, I acknowledge that I did not always have this humility.

Both my adultery and the accumulation of continuous debt humbled me. I could come from nowhere but the lowest point of my life anytime I ever spoke to anyone. I always had to serve them from wherever I was at the time. I had nothing to give other than myself as I was, and God was working through me.

Proverbs 13:10

Pride leads to arguments; be humble, take advice, and become wise.

I was able to minister from that point, and to be used by God. To be a little bit wiser than before. All the glory is given to Him, and knowing that it was nothing from me, but it was all Him that made this possible: it was from this that I was able to begin to truly be a pastor.

Humility served me better than shame or arrogance, but I didn't think in those terms in earlier years. God could never have used "the old Tim." I was too proud. I was too arrogant. I was 100% ego driven. Pretending to be independent, all the while in bondage.

From humility, I learned to walk in others' shoes. I developed empathy for their situations. I could think before I spoke. I could remember that God always wanted me to see my helplessness, for He is the answer—not some manmade solution. We are to live life and do life with God. We can't call on Him like some cosmic Santa Clause to give us what we want.

No. Every day I walk with Him. He leads. I follow.

James 1:2–8

> [2] *Consider it pure joy, my brothers and sisters, whenever you face trials of many kinds,*
>
> [3] *because you know that the testing of your faith produces perseverance.*
>
> [4] *Let perseverance finish its work so that you may be mature and complete, not lacking anything.*
>
> [5] *If any of you lacks wisdom, you should ask God, who gives generously to all without finding fault, and it will be given to you.*
>
> [6] *But when you ask, you must believe and not doubt, because the one who doubts is like a wave of the sea, blown and tossed by the wind.*
>
> [7] *That person should not expect to receive anything from the Lord.*
>
> [8] *Such a person is double-minded and unstable in all they do.*

I am in a relationship with Him. My talks with Him are two-way conversations—listening, obeying, performing, asking, and again listening. Falling down. Getting up again. Facing bigger challenges with trust and faith. Making progress with Him guiding me.

CHAPTER FOUR

———

Chasing Sex and Other Addictions

Addiction is an Ego Veil Hiding God from Your Life

It's hard to verbalize how powerless and how helpless I felt when facing temptation and the compulsion to act out.

I was exposed to pornography in magazines as a child with other boys in our little clubhouse (one of the boys had the literature; then I found some in my parents' house). I was later subjected to inappropriate fondling by a childcare provider's daughter. I resorted to masturbation as a cure to ease my pain. I objectified women. Like a lot of men, I'd give a number or letter grade to categorize how I found women, judging them to be a 6 or a 2 or an A or a D.

I grew up in a very segregated town with a population of about 2,500. I ran with white friends and did school sports with white guys, but we black guys could not overtly date white girls. That was not generally accepted. I succumbed to the push/pull of the black/white race issue. There is a lot more I could say about this issue. It is best left alone, perhaps, for now. Suffice it to say, I was deep in that black/white condition, consciously, subconsciously, and unable to date who I cared about in a healthy way.

Bondage

This is how I fell into the bondage of lust.

It all started early in my childhood. I would say around age five or six years of age when I was at a babysitter's house. We had several different babysitters growing up. My parents both worked and I know that their wish was to provide the best care possible. There was one particular babysitter that I went to where the girl was several years older than me, and I believe that I was looking for "love."

Later, after much counseling, I realized that my relationship with my father was one from which I was always seeking approval and not perceiving that I was receiving it. Well, in this situation, I and the babysitter's daughter—who was several years older than me—would often find ourselves alone. She and I did what kids do—show each other body parts and so forth. She and I would go into progressive touching and kissing and laying on each other and touching each other in inappropriate areas.

I've come to believe that she must have been abused earlier in her life or had things done to her that she was just mimicking. I say this because she wasn't that much older than me. She wasn't an adult yet. We would often find ourselves engaged in some little sexual innuendos, but never with any sexual penetration or anything like that. Just contact and hiding under beds or behind doors or outside.

I looked and longed for those situations, and went there to feel loved and appreciated. It escalated until one day her mother caught us in a peculiar situation. After that was when I began to spur on my desire for females and to look for some type of sexual touch.

In the Song of Solomon, it talks about not looking to excite that love or lust early in life because it is a very powerful and seductive love that God has in store for those who are married that keeps them connected to one another. When we elicit that love early on, it can corrupt us. It did for me.

From there, this situation progressed. Then, around age eight or nine, the neighborhood boys invited me to their club. We had a "club" out in the middle of a field, and we just dubbed it our own place. One day, I was invited to that location, and a guy shared a stash of pornography magazines that he had obviously found in his father's things. From time to time, we would go back to the club and look at those magazines and images. They began to be seared into my memory.

Then eventually I found my own father's pornography in our house. I was maybe 10 or 11 at that time. In that location, we may have been playing hide-and-seek in our house and I stumbled upon a book or two underneath the bed. It provided me the opportunity to go back, look, and drink in those pictures. Sometimes I would even try it when people were in the house. I would make it my mission to look and not get caught. I'd risk getting in trouble. That was the beginning of the pull that it had on me.

It was a growing power in my life. It didn't make any sense, but more and more I wanted to look at it. Sometimes when the family was gone, I could just lay in there and look and read the stories. I began to read and create a fantasy in my mind of how I could manipulate and control those situations. I didn't know anything about orgasms or anything at that time; it was just constantly building a lust in my head and storing away pictures in my mind that I could recall any time I chose to. It began to create just those things in my head.

There were other times and situations where I heard people speaking about women in a derogatory manner. I remember one time a fill-in parent for our Boy Scout activity said that all sex was good, just some is better than others. I didn't understand what that meant, but that comment stayed with me for the longest time.

Then, as I turned 11 or 12, right around junior high, masturbation and addiction started in a much stronger way. I think I had my first wet dream and didn't understand what that was all about or how it even happened. I remember feeling just so exhilarated, but I also felt shame about what was going on with me. But I was still looking for those opportunities when I could find magazines in the house or go to a friend's house and look at some.

Then one day I realized, as guys were talking, what masturbation was and how I could control it myself. That began a long series of trying to masturbate. I shared a room with my brother. How to do that and not get caught was the focus. It was mostly at night. I was peculiar in that I had a dry humping type process that I did, instead of a manual hands stimulation to myself. It was always that challenge of pushing something to the edge and not getting caught. This escalated into times when I was at the swimming pool and trying to touch or grab girls that were in the water. It became like a game that we played with the females at the pool. There was a ring of people that always got involved. It was just mischievous behavior. There was constant talk about who you could mess with and who you couldn't.

As I grew up, there was this constant awkward tension about who you could date and who you couldn't date. I was a black guy growing up in a predominantly white community. There was always that tension about who I wanted to date versus who I knew I could date. I was always suppressing my desire to be involved with a girl that I liked. All through my childhood there was always this tension of wanting to date the girl of my liking who might happen to be white, I guess, and not being able to.

That all changed when I went to college. In 1986, I attended the University of Missouri, Columbia. It was kind of like a gold fish being released into the Pacific Ocean. There were thousands upon thousands of females there. There was this one perch in Lowry Mall where my buddies and I would just sit and look at women and, during the day, just get drunk with the people that walked by. That's when I started masturbating during my college years. That led to what I would consider a situation where I discovered what I called "seductive women" and the magnetic look you could share with some people and understand that they, too, shared that same bent toward sexual sin and the double-mind-edness that came with that.

Later in my freshman year I had a conversation with my mother, where I expressed an emptiness—a blah and depressed feeling. My mom asked me if I had been going to church, and I said no. She recommended I get involved with some type of church or ministry on campus. I did, and that's when I started with a Christian group on campus. It was a Bible study that was teaching you how to share your testimony, evangelize people, and memorize scripture. In that situation it happened almost instantly—there was this girl that was attracted to me, and I didn't know it. One night after Bible study, she invited me over to her dorm room, and I said, "Sure." We were going to study some more together.

As I remember it, I went up to her room and we were studying for a short period of time. Then she turned the lights out. As she turned the lights out, she took her clothes off and reached for me to come over to her. I realized what was going to transpire as she began to undress me. The next thing I knew, we were under the covers in her bedroom. She had a single room. She was much older than me—she was 26 and I was 19. She had her way with me that evening. That was the first time I had any real type of sexual experience with a woman. Prior to that, it was just inappropriate touching. That evening it escalated into sexual intercourse for me for the first time. After that, I knew that it was something that I shouldn't have done. There was the fear of, "Oh wow, had she gotten pregnant? What was going on?" I wasn't supposed to do that, but also, there was the exhilaration of touching and feeling her body in a way that I never had with a woman before. There was a God conflict going on in my head at the same time. How could I be having sexual relations with someone from my Bible group and not know that wasn't acceptable? Wasn't I breaking a commandment? Or sinning against God?

In that situation, we knew that we should not have done what we did. She immediately felt shame and didn't want to meet. But time after time we would get together and be praying or memorizing scripture and find ourselves connected again. This led to many dysfunctional times I won't even go into here.

This escalated into seeking women for sexual contact. It erupted numerous times while I was in college. It escalated more and more, to the point where I would go out and look, sit, watch and get drunk with women, then go back to masturbate in my dorm room, sometimes six or seven times a day. This escalated into an uncontrollable compulsion and a cycle of shame. It began with resisting, knowing that I didn't want to commit the sexual misconduct, but it was accompanied by an understanding that the release it gave me brought calmness and peacefulness that allowed me to cope with the rest of my day. In college, I dated two girls for a longer period of time, but was still seeking out other girls and fantasizing about sexual relations with some of them.

It carried on in this way until I met my wife in college. One day, I went to visit my cousin to have her review my English paper since she was an English major. There was this girl in her room, and they were in a graduate dorm, and I noticed her as she was telling her story about how she couldn't find a good guy. She was talking about her experience that summer in dating, and how she was not having any luck finding a guy who was nice to her and would be kind to her. In my mind, I was saying, I could be a nice guy to her. I could be a nice guy. She was very beautiful and appealing to me, but of course, at that time, she did not recognize me. I was younger than her, and I was not sure she was even interested in me. I was a black guy. She was a white girl.

Later that evening, I called her and asked her out on a date. She accepted, and that was the beginning of our time together. That evening, after we went on our date, I saw a golden halo around her head, and for whatever reason, it set in my spirit that this is the woman that I would marry. I went back and told my college roommate, "Hey, I met the woman that I'm going to marry," and he said, "Oh, Tim, just be quiet and go to bed."

It evolved into a relationship. She left maybe three months later and started her practicum in social work, teaching in a school setting. We were separated during that time. This was my senior year in college. I graduated that year and went off to Officer Basic Training in Alabama. She came down and visited me once. Later that summer, I decided to propose to her on her birthday and did so. We were married that Christmas Eve, 1990.

I thought that being in a marriage would solve my problem. I would no longer be panicking, convulsing, and masturbating to release the tension. I believe one of the biggest deceptions people with sexual sin and addictions believe is that "When I get married, I'll have endless sex, and I won't have that problem." Probably for the first three or four years that was true. Everything reduced and we had a wonderful and loving relationship, but I was always fighting the battles in my mind with the good guy/bad guy stress and always running to masturbation every time I was stressed.

Things went well on the whole for several years until there was a tipping point for me. It was after we had our older daughter and the twins. That also was when my wife stopped participating with me in business activities.

I don't think this new family pressure was a real issue. It felt more like my closest business partner had abandoned me. I felt stress from her decision without knowing it at the time. I didn't know how to move forward. I felt incomplete without her by my side in my business life. But, again, I didn't consciously recognize this as part of my issues till later years. At the time, it affected how I coped with things, where we went and what we did. I struggled back and forth for many years from then on, just with pornography. I remember one time I had begun to store some of it in the house on videos and left it out on the bed before I went to work. My wife was calling me in a rage, wanting to know what was going on and what was this filth that I had brought into the house. That made me just dive deeper underground, so to speak. I hid my material from then on. The deviousness of my mind had me start covering up my tracks and living a double-minded life.

I wanted to tell her what my problem was, but I feared she wouldn't stay with me if she knew what a vile and double-minded person I was with an addiction to pornography and a deeply ingrained problem with masturbation.

This grew and escalated for several years, and I had changed jobs. I was in a job where I came in contact with the public on a daily basis.

I think there's always this magnetic attraction phenomenon known to men who are addicted, that you have with other people. You can just look at some women and understand that they, too, carry that same seductive connection. I don't know what you want to call it, but there's a sexual energy that seems to radiate around a person. You can look at them and there's a two or three-second look with a magnetic connection between your spirit and their spirit. You know there can be more if you take it there. If you open your mouth and start a conversation, it's all over. You are in the cycle that is never ending, where you're fighting yourself in your head. On the inside, you know if you continue having a conversation with her, it's going to lead you into a precarious situation where the two of you might come together.

The Bible tells us in Joseph's story that the thing to do is to turn immediately, without thought, and to flee. Multiple passages, primarily in Proverbs Chapter 7 tell us not to be connected or fall into the seductive ways of women because it leads to death. I would fight this advice time and time again.

In one extended adulterous relationship, I was entangled in such a way. I was consistently going back into it instead of fleeing it. I had approached this woman who was working in my office and shared with her the appreciation and affection I had for her. I manipulated the situation, no doubt. It was the beginning of my seduction of her. I was no longer having the battle between good and bad in my head—the bad won. At this point in the addiction, your conscious is seared. You have abandoned God, and by refusal to turn to God, He leaves you to your depravity. That is what happened to me.

The beginning of all downfalls is when you express the love or admiration you have for an inappropriate person or situation to the other person. That is the beginning of your downfall and the bondage that ensues.

Over a period of time, it developed into a sexual relationship in which I abandoned all thought or reason. I abandoned running my business with any real consciousness. I was caught up in the passion of lust. It nearly destroyed both our families. Had her husband not tape recorded a conversation we had, I do not know if I ever would have made it out of that situation alive. That was the impetus that made me confess to my wife what had happened.

This occurred on a Friday night, and I refused to take Communion on the following Sunday. I wanted to be the person to tell my wife about the affair before she heard it from anyone else, but I was racked with the possibility that she would divorce me and that I would never see my children again. That fear was always there, keeping me from being honest with her and confessing my sin. There was a flurry of crazy thoughts that went through my head, which are better left out of this story.

In the end, I did confess that relationship to my wife, and that is what started me on the road to recovery.

She was enraged. I never thought she would respond in the way she eventually did. Later, she told me that God came to her with a resounding voice, saying to her, "Help him. Help him. Help him."

She, being a social worker, knew that some of the probable help I could get was attending a 12-step program called Sexaholics Anonymous. I never even knew such a program existed, but in trying to hold my marriage together and keep my children, I would have agreed to anything. I started attending those S.A. meetings one or two times a week to gain sanity. I found out that many of the things I had done were wrong, as were the ways I dealt with them. I had dumped the situation on my children immediately after admitting it to my wife. I pulled off the side of the road as we were driving home and asked them to forgive me. Had I thought clearly, I'd've seen they were at an age far too young for them to understand or bear the consequences.

With hindsight, I realize I wasn't in the right frame of mind or taking the right action with my kids. I do know, also by looking back, that speaking it out to them helped me begin a journey of walking out of addiction.

Recovery Begins

In the beginning, there was a lot of knuckling down. I had recovery but not sobriety, as they say in this field. I white-knuckled a lot. It wasn't smooth sailing by any means.

This is the recovery process—my personal rehab process—that has been underway since that time over ten years ago. People with addictions commonly encounter triggers in their life that will send them rolling back to a prior point in their life. Common triggers include loneliness, anger, sadness, fear, fatigue, tension, despair, and feeling unappreciated, unloved, or disapproved of. Sometimes that trigger will send us back into a situation where we're looking to get a quick solution to that problem.

Triggers often become sexualized, meaning that the person understands they're feeling this way. The pressure that they're living under creates anxiety. This anxiety, over time, is linked to a sexual acting out, and in that sexual acting out, the person understands that they're relieved from the stress but that it's a temporary fix.

It's kind of like a drug of choice. The challenge is that you carry your drug of choice with you all the time because you have the mental pictures stored away in your mind that can be recalled at any moment. It's kind of like Pavlov's dog—when triggers cause some difficult or painful feelings, the person is motivated into a sexual act and the anticipation of the positive mood change they're going to create.

What happens is that you go to that drug of choice and it "medicates" and relieves the body— temporarily. Researchers have found that the chemical called dopamine is what medicates you. It's a kind of kick to the body, and now this sexual addiction causes the body to need more and more of the drug called dopamine because over time it has a diminishing effect on the body. You find yourself going deeper into the addiction. You must do riskier and crazier things to even feel the new fix of the drug and its high.

It creates more emotional pain, not less. You're constantly crying out for healing on the inside, but you're believing what Satan has told you. Satan told the lie that this short-term fix will solve the problem, and you will lose it all if you tell anyone about it. It does solve the problem temporarily, but it creates such a cycle of emotional challenges that the body goes back to craving the feeling over and over again for a solution.

Satan doesn't tell us that it's never a long-term answer to what you're looking for. It's basically shame and, as we know from the Garden of Eden, once God revealed to them their desire for lust, shame was what came in, and they recognized they were naked and afraid.

In order for you to be set free from this stronghold, it calls for two components to be in place. One component is what's necessary to solve the spiritual need and the other one is the work needed to correct the natural physical need and behaviors.

It is important to recognize the self-deception that one's marriage is going to solve the problems. It doesn't solve any problems. That is what I looked for, in spite of that truth. What happens is that as one looks at pornography, it begins to tell you that you need a variety of sexual partners and that variety will solve the problem. It's certainly not true, but it is one of the beliefs that comes with a craving for pornography. The wiring in the brain becomes addicted to the drug of choice that it helps emit. Marriage doesn't solve the situation.

Also important is not to believe that prayer alone can solve the problem. Prayer is a very important portion of it, but prayer alone will not solve the problem. Prayer is vital to bringing the mind under control and renewing its thought patterns. You can't always stay in the kneeling position praying constantly (I found myself both wishing I could and hoping I couldn't).

Related to prayer is belief that reading the Bible alone will solve your problem. The Bible is the source of all answers and it is definitely the foundation to build your life upon. It provides hope. It provides direction. It shows you the way to follow. But once again, you can't be reading all the time. Prayer and reading the Bible in unison with Christian counseling can bring the answer and a surrender to God's guidance.

The natural and behavioral practices have to be in unison with the practices of prayer and Bible study. You have to learn an alternative way of dealing with life and substituting that physical behavior with something else. We have been speaking of this bondage we're in—living in an environment where we begin to learn how to live in healthy relationships and learning how to face those childhood issues that allowed you to run to the drug as a short-term solution to your problems. As you begin your recovery, you must be careful because your issue can morph into some other addiction. A sex addiction can transform itself into a food addiction, an activity addition, alcoholism, or workaholism. You have to alter the situation and resolve your problem from within a healthy environment. You must learn how to recognize the challenges and triggers and the solutions you use to solve the emotional and spiritual problem that is evident in your life.

Prayer, Bible study and fasting will help you face this spiritual condition, but you also have to learn how to live in relationship with yourself, with your Lord, and with those around you. All these approaches and tools go hand in hand with having someone to talk to who is skilled and trained in how to address these situations in your life (Christian counsellor; accountability partner).

It took around four years of counseling before Nancy and I were able to communicate in a way that wasn't damaging to us or others around us. We spent three years having our girls go through counseling so they could be adjusted and have a proper image of who men are and can be in their life, and also seeing their own self-esteem and understanding who they are as God's children.

The last three years have been, for me, understanding the message the Lord wants me to share and bring to my fellow man and how we can give hope to other marriages encountering this situation. As we talk with people, often one on one, we find it's a widespread situation—America has been so sexualized, and the messages have become very distorted. It was a struggle for me, I don't deny it. It is today an ongoing struggle that I deal with, but I am so much further along than where I was as a young adult growing up. My wife has had a tremendous challenge placed on her in being married to me. We walk this out daily, together.

It's a struggle, yes. The battle is on every single day. This is nothing you get past completely and can look back at and never again have a problem with. I believe this is something you are constantly dealing with and you must be on your guard against its reappearance. You call out to the Lord for strength on a regular and continual basis. You learn ways to overcome it, through His Guidance. For me, now, that comes mostly by helping other people as I continue to learn, to teach and to walk through it. As I do, I gain a better understanding of how to be strong.

The Solutions I Found

This is the recovery plan, the answer to the sexual sin challenge. This came from James MacDonald's "Jesus Confronts Sexual Sin Part B." Sexual sin always drags you down to death.

To start out in your recovery, you have to make some changes. They involve your home environment and your communication habits. You now have to ban things you formerly tolerated without thinking about them.

There are five things tolerated in a Christian home that should not be:

- One is explicit movies, DVDs, or anything with sexual scenes depicted.

- Two is cable channels and Internet that is unblocked or unfiltered.

- Three is unaccountable time; you want to know the whereabouts of your family members. Report your schedule to loved ones. Create boundaries with the opposite sex in meals and travel. Plan to be a godly man and be that man. Create a system of accountability.

- Four is secretive relationships. When you have a phone call, put it on speaker so that your spouse can hear at all times.

- Five is opposite sex friendships—definitely not. Anyone that you know of the opposite sex needs to be introduced to your spouse so that she can become friends with them. Then you can communicate with them together.

There is a story in Revelations Chapter 2: 18–29:

[18] To the angel of the church in Thyatira write: These are the words of the Son of God, whose eyes are like blazing fire and whose feet are like burnished bronze.

[19] I know your deeds, your love and faith, your service and perseverance, and that you are now doing more than you did at first.

[20] Nevertheless, I have this against you: You tolerate that woman Jezebel, who calls herself a prophet. By her teaching, she misleads my servants into sexual immorality and the eating of food sacrificed to idols.

[21] I have given her time to repent of her immorality, but she is unwilling.

[22] So I will cast her on a bed of suffering, and I will make those who commit adultery with her suffer intensely, unless they repent of her ways.

[23] I will strike her children dead. Then all the churches will know that I am he who searches hearts and minds, and I will repay each of you according to your deeds.

[24] Now I say to the rest of you in Thyatira, to you who do not hold to her teaching and have not learned Satan's so-called deep secrets, 'I will not impose any other burden on you,

[25] except to hold on to what you have until I come.

[26] To the one who is victorious and does my will to the end, I will give authority over the nations—

27 that one 'will rule them with an iron scepter and will dash them to pieces like pottery'—just as I have received authority from my Father.

28 I will also give that one the morning star.

29 Whoever has ears, let them hear what the Spirit says to the churches.

It talks about Jezebel and how she created a connection between sensuality and spirituality, saying you can do anything you want sexually with your body and still be considered a Christian. Jesus was chastising the church that He sent the letter to and said that was wrong. In order to change and to be released from the addiction, the first step is repentance. It is the cure for sexual sin. Change your mind, change your direction. Verses that talk about the things that need to happen to truly know that you have repented would be Luke 3: 8 and Acts 26: 20.

Luke 3: 8

8 Produce fruit in keeping with repentance. And do not begin to say to yourselves, 'We have Abraham as our father.' For I tell you that out of these stones God can raise up children for Abraham.

Acts 26: 20

20 First to those in Damascus, then to those in Jerusalem and in all Judea, and then to the Gentiles, I preached that they should repent and turn to God and demonstrate their repentance by their deeds.

There are five things that must be done. Then you will know that you have truly repented.

- Number one is open confession of sin. No more hiding the problems. Make a male-to-male confession and a female-to-female confession. Refer to James 5:16:

   16 Therefore confess your sins to each other and pray for each other so that you may be healed. The prayer of a righteous person is powerful and effective.

- Number two, the absence of all rationalization. That's where the mind tries to justify all your actions. Take personal responsibility.

- Number three, restoration. Make it right with the people that you have injured. Go and seek them out. This is about apology and forgiveness.

- Number four, a restored heart for God. No more blocking God. No more feeling like you can't go to church, read the word, or pray. That begins to melt away.

- Number five, accountability for change. Filter the computer. Put a plan in place. Involve two or three other men and hold each other's feet to the fire to win.

What's it going to look like in order to do that? You're going to have to lose your pride. You'll have to walk in shame for a while, but God does not walk away from you. When you are in the spirit of shame, it's that very brokenness that He can then begin to work out of you. That's what He's looking for, a broken and contrite heart. That's when He knows that He has got your attention, and you are willing to try it His way!

But what if you refuse to repent? The Lord says later in the passage that when Jezebel refused to repent, He was going to bring on severe tribulation, "Behold that I will throw her into a sickbed." God brings sickness to the sexually immoral as an inducement to repent and change their ways. I wonder how much sickness God has brought on in a form of judgment on the sexually immoral.

It also talks about Him being in a vice or pressure. Also, in Proverbs, it talks about how you will lose those things. You will walk in shame. Your wealth will be gone. Someone else will take it and sickness will overcome you. Is it worth losing it all just to keep your pride?

Proverbs 5: 9–11

> *⁹ lest you lose your honor to others and your dignity to one who is cruel,*
>
> *¹⁰ lest strangers feast on your wealth and your toil enrich the house of another.*
>
> *¹¹ At the end of your life you will groan, when your flesh and body are spent.*

In 1 Corinthians 6: 18 it talks about how we sin against our own body and it helps to separate us from God:

> *¹⁸ Flee from sexual immorality. All other sins a person commits are outside the body, but whoever sins sexually, sins against their own body.*

Revelation 2: 23 says, "I will strike her children dead." Do we know if that's her literal children or not? We don't know, but He promises that. But the world says that sexual fantasy, lust, sexual romping and getting into bed with everybody is just enjoyment and entertainment. God says that that is reserved just for our marriage, and when we do not abide by His rules, there are consequences.

Here's what we know. If you go down a road, it leads somewhere specific. Certain roads lead to certain places. The road of sexual sin always, always leads to self-destruction. It will destroy you. It will addict you. It will drag you down to death and to hell itself. That road always goes to the same place, no matter what the mind says. At the end of Proverbs, it tells us in chapter 5 and chapter 7 that when we follow the seductive woman, it leads to a snare like a deer about to be killed. It will lead us to death. In Revelation 2: 25 the Lord tells us to stand strong. Stand and wait until He comes again. Keep His commands and He will give us rule and authority over the nations. He tells us there's a reward if we're vigilant about keeping ourselves pure—that we will receive the Morning Star. Jesus Himself is the Morning Star.

Now, in conclusion, let's say you've decided that "This is the path that I want to go. I want to repent." Christian therapist Dr. Mark Laaser always asks these three spiritual questions to his people struggling with sexual issues.

• Number one: Do you want to get well?

Read in the Bible about the man Christ healed in John 5:1–9. Christ asks a very important question of this man. This question is core to our healing. He asked, "Do you want to be healed?" The fellow had been stuck for 38 years!

How long have you been stuck? How deep is your motivation for healing? Are you willing to change? Don't say you are if you aren't. If you don't want to heal, it is not going to happen.

• Number two: What are you thirsty for?

Read the story of the woman Christ met at the well one day, found in chapter 4 of John. Obviously, sexuality had been a false solution for her real needs as a woman.

How has sexuality been a false solution for you, for your true needs? Has there ever been a time when sexually acting out, whether overt sexual practices has satisfied you for more than thirty seconds? How did your sexual issues interfere with your relationship with your spouse? What are you thirsty for?

• Number three: What are you willing to die for?

In chapter 11 of John, Christ attended the funeral of a man who would not have died if Christ had arrived a little sooner. In this story, we confront our selfishness as we read about Lazarus' death.

The deepest issue of sexual healing is often sacrifice. Would you die for your children, your country? How about your spouse? What has to die inside you for you to live refreshed? What false sexual activity, whether overt or covert, will you need to give up to experience true connection and intimacy?

Prayer for Salvation

I guess here I have to put my minister's hat on.

I'm sure there are many reading this book who have heard of Jesus but have no idea how to bring Jesus Christ into their life, or who He could be for them. I've included many Bible verses and a lot of scripture in my story. I have been a believer throughout this rehabbing process of mine, and have called massively on the Word to guide me.

The situation of sin and addiction doesn't just touch Christians; it touches everyone. Not everyone may know how to tap into the power of Jesus Christ that is present for us all. Understand this: Jesus Christ died so that all of our sins could be forgiven. Every single one. Many people believe that they are too far lost, or have committed a sin too atrocious for God to forgive. That is never true. The Christ died on the cross so that everyone may have the opportunity to know and live in a relationship with Him.

The first step for us is to turn away from our sins and repent for what we've done. That's the first step that we have to take. We must recognize the sin for what it is, give it up, and ask for forgiveness.

The next thing we have to do is recognize that God created us for a relationship—to be in union with Him. We have to come back into a personal union with God. We have to believe that Jesus Christ paid the penalty for our sins. One time, He paid it for us all. He died upon the cross. He rose from the dead. He had victory over death. We have to admit to Him that we are a sinful person. We must ask for forgiveness and turn our life and the control of it over to the Lord Jesus Christ. We do this so that He can begin to show us the way and walk with us through the challenging parts of our life, and also to help us understand. We come back into a union with Him. We begin to hear and understand His Word and be obedient to it as well as His directives and the commandments that He gives us.

He is much kinder, gentler and more graceful than any human person we could probably ever imagine. We may think that we do not even have the right to ask for a second chance from Him, but He is the God of second chances, third chances … and fourth chances. He never gives up on us. He is a God of mercy who extends love and compassion to us at a time when we are the most broken and needful of His love and understanding.

If you have not asked God to come into your heart, it's a simple process. Asking for salvation— asking to be rescued from bondage and to recover from old behaviors—is nothing complicated. You could even begin with a short prayer like this:

> *"Oh God, I am a sinner. I am sorry for my sin. I want to turn away from my sin. Please forgive me. I believe Jesus Christ is Your Son. I believe He died on a cross for my sin, and You raised Him to life. I want to trust Him as my Savior and follow Him as my Lord from this day forward, forever more. Lord, I put my trust in You and surrender my life to You. Please come into my life and fill me with Your Holy Spirit. In Jesus' name. Amen."*

It's as simple as that. If you prayed this prayer, please contact us. Now, begin to travel with Him down the road to freedom from bondage. Once you've said that prayer, you need to contact a local church or someone you know that attends a church, and share your decision with them. Begin by getting into a small group, and study the Word. Become a student of Jesus Christ. Little by little, day by day, you will feel the impact of His guidance and gain more understanding about what it looks like to follow someone who has all the answers and all the power to transform you from the situation of sin and double-mindedness you find yourself in.

Speaking out about Lust

1 John 2:16

> *[16] For everything in the world—the lust of the flesh, the lust of the eyes, and the pride of life—comes not from the Father but from the world.*

Three or four years into my recovery, as I grew more confident in my sermon writing and my delivery of the Word to my congregation, the Lord moved me to do something that I did not want to do. I needed to present a sermon on lust. I had to talk about this publicly in front of my congregation. This is the sermon that I shared with my congregation, and it might have been more healing for me than a revelation for them.

I have said it, "You can't teach what you don't know. You can't lead others where you won't go." I knew lust in more than one of its forms! Letting go of Satan's lust temptations is like peeling back the layers of an onion … It seems never ending, but there is an end. Since I discovered a solution to the problem, through the study of the Word and prayer and fasting, I wanted to share how it all started. I wanted to speak about Lust.

So I thought about it. Lust. A short-term fix. A mental degradation. Mind spinning round and round until that itch is scratched. Manipulation of others; the mind manipulating me. Being thrown into isolation and anxiety. Double-mindedness. To get temporarily free of all that pain, what do we do but go along with Lust! We cave in. And we are back, full circle, to the short-term fix. We nod at this description when we are talking about drug addicts, but drug users are far from the only lust-driven addictions we humans know.

Lust is an appetite that cannot be filled. "More, more, more," doesn't solve the pain, but Satan tries to tell us it does. Satan cannot fill us up. Satan cannot fulfill us, nor the substitutes we try to use in place of God. God is the only true answer to that hole in our soul.

At that time, we were living in one of our rentals. I had lost everything in bankruptcy proceedings. We had moved from our first home that we had built to a home I had purchased to be a rental for some income.

I can't express how many (thousand?) times I have read Proverbs chapter 5. I balanced the challenge of "keeping to a path far from her" by remembering to "drink water from my own cistern"—to be with my wife, not the other man's. I was in full view of the Lord and was only kidding myself that I was hidden from

His sight. But in the end I saw that I was the woman in the story, leading others away from the Lord!

My oldest daughter Kayla, at age 11 or so, copied the verses below and gave them to me, saying, "Dad, you need this!"

Proverbs 5: 15–23

> [15] *Drink water from your own cistern, running water from your own well.*
>
> [16] *Should your springs overflow in the streets,*
>
> [17] *Let them be yours alone, never to be shared with strangers.*
>
> [18] *May your fountain be blessed, and may you rejoice in the wife of your youth.*
>
> [19] *A loving doe, a graceful deer—may her breasts satisfy you always, may you ever be intoxicated with her love.*
>
> [20] *Why, my son, be intoxicated with another man's wife? Why embrace the bosom of a wayward woman?*
>
> [21] *For your ways are in full view of the LORD, and he examines all your paths.*
>
> [22] *The evil deeds of the wicked ensnare them; the cords of their sins hold them fast.*
>
> [23] *For lack of discipline they will die, led astray by their own great folly.*

You are looking for the Messiah and He is right here! He is within you. You only need to reach out (from within yourself) to Him. Walk in Faith that He is within you. Know that Love is His truth. Know that Lust is the lie of Satan.

In addition to Proverbs chapter 5 was the Parable of the Woman at the Well. There I learned to drink the water of Jesus, not the water of Satan.

John 4: 3–32

> [3] *So he left Judea and went back once more to Galilee.*
>
> [4] *Now he had to go through Samaria.*

⁵ *So he came to a town in Samaria called Sychar, near the plot of ground Jacob had given to his son Joseph.*

⁶ *Jacob's well was there, and Jesus, tired as he was from the journey, sat down by the well. It was about noon.*

⁷ *When a Samaritan woman came to draw water, Jesus said to her, "Will you give me a drink?"*

⁸ *(His disciples had gone into the town to buy food.)*

⁹ *The Samaritan woman said to him, "You are a Jew and I am a Samaritan woman. How can you ask me for a drink?" (For Jews do not associate with Samaritans.)*

¹⁰ *Jesus answered her, "If you knew the gift of God and who it is that asks you for a drink, you would have asked him and he would have given you living water."*

¹¹ *"Sir," the woman said, "you have nothing to draw with and the well is deep. Where can you get this living water?*

¹² *Are you greater than our father Jacob, who gave us the well and drank from it himself, as did also his sons and his livestock?"*

¹³ *Jesus answered, "Everyone who drinks this water will be thirsty again,*

¹⁴ *but whoever drinks the water I give them will never thirst. Indeed, the water I give them will become in them a spring of water welling up to eternal life."*

¹⁵ *The woman said to him, "Sir, give me this water so that I won't get thirsty and have to keep coming here to draw water."*

¹⁶ *He told her, "Go, call your husband and come back."*

¹⁷ *"I have no husband," she replied. Jesus said to her, "You are right when you say you have no husband.*

¹⁸ *The fact is, you have had five husbands, and the man you now have is not your husband. What you have just said is quite true."*

¹⁹ *"Sir," the woman said, "I can see that you are a prophet.*

²⁰ *Our ancestors worshiped on this mountain, but you Jews claim that the place where we must worship is in Jerusalem."*

²¹ *"Woman," Jesus replied, "believe me, a time is coming when you will worship the Father neither on this mountain nor in Jerusalem.*

²² You Samaritans worship what you do not know; we worship what we do know, for salvation is from the Jews.

²³ Yet a time is coming and has now come when the true worshipers will worship the Father in the Spirit and in truth, for they are the kind of worshipers the Father seeks.

²⁴ God is spirit, and his worshipers must worship in the Spirit and in truth."

²⁵ The woman said, "I know that the Messiah (called Christ) is coming. When he comes, he will explain everything to us."

²⁶ Then Jesus declared, "I, the one speaking to you—I am he."

²⁷ Just then his disciples returned and were surprised to find him talking with a woman. But no one asked, "What do you want?" or "Why are you talking with her?"

²⁸ Then, leaving her water jar, the woman went back to the town and said to the people,

²⁹ "Come, see a man who told me everything I ever did. Could this be the Messiah?"

³⁰ They came out of the town and made their way toward him.

³¹ Meanwhile his disciples urged him, "Rabbi, eat something."

³² But he said to them, "I have food to eat that you know nothing about."

Love is from God. Lust is from Satan. How can we know the difference?

Satan's "divide and conquer" approach uses Lust of the body and Lust of the eye. By using the body and mind's lust as a distraction for us from the Lord's Path, we certainly can look away from God and stop hearing Him.

We act from compulsions: lust for this or that achievement; lust for this or that consumer item that catches our eye; lust for what this or that neighbor has that we do not; lust for easy wealth; lust for the neighbor's wife. We want something, but once we have it, we find ourselves still "thirsty."

We want what we cannot or do not have, yet having it is not satisfying. So it is with carnal lust; lust for money, lust for fame and notoriety and success. We are looking in the wrong place for our satiation, for our fulfillment.

And we lust for struggle! Doesn't that sound odd? Struggle is created by Satan. Effortless living is given to us by the Lord. I just wasn't seeing that.

To enter the ministry, the Lord admonished me to release thinking that "not working for my living" meant not having a living. I fought that. I struggled internally with my Lord to keep on with business. He kept saying, "No." I was not fulfilled in business or with the money I made. Not the way I was going about it, at least.

But I learned that the Lord provides—tuition for my kids, vehicles, and $5000 in an account when I needed that amount to meet payroll, which shouldn't have been there by all our calculations. To this day it remains unexplained. The Lord brought the people I needed to be with in order to learn compassion and to learn how to pour into others in need. He brought the books and the mentors and the coaches I needed to learn about business. He created circumstances and events that taught me to fast, and then he brought a methodology to achieve it.

I could never have put an ad in the local paper and been provided with any of this. The Lord provided. The Lord fulfilled my needs. He fulfilled me once I let Him in.

The woman in the Scripture kept going back to Satan's trap. God sets you free of that trap. You never need to go back because He fills you from within daily. But it is a daily choice. We can wage war with Satan daily, or walk in the way of the Holy Spirit.

Walk out of your self-made prison and be free. Drop all your baggage. Drop all your emotional, spiritual, and financial baggage. That was the first step for me.

The second step for me of God's directive was set the captives free. Help those around me who came to me for assistance, and help them drink the water of Christ.

What do you need to be free of? The Lord said, It doesn't matter—be free of it all, with Me.

Galatians 5:16–26

[16] *So I say, walk by the Spirit, and you will not gratify the desires of the flesh.*

[17] *For the flesh desires what is contrary to the Spirit, and the Spirit what is contrary to the flesh. They are in conflict with each other, so that you are not to do whatever you want.*

[18] *But if you are led by the Spirit, you are not under the law.*

[19] *The acts of the flesh are obvious: sexual immorality, impurity and debauchery;*

[20] *idolatry and witchcraft; hatred, discord, jealousy, fits of rage, selfish ambition, dissensions, factions*

[21] *and envy; drunkenness, orgies, and the like. I warn you, as I did before, that those who live like this will not inherit the kingdom of God.*

[22] *But the fruit of the Spirit is love, joy, peace, forbearance, kindness, goodness, faithfulness,*

[23] *gentleness and self-control. Against such things there is no law.*

[24] *Those who belong to Christ Jesus have crucified the flesh with its passions and desires.*

[25] *Since we live by the Spirit, let us keep in step with the Spirit.*

[26] *Let us not become conceited, provoking and envying each other.*

CHAPTER FIVE

—

Put Your Life in Order

For years and years, I thought my life had pretty good order. Nancy worked a predictable job and schedule, with predictable pay. The girls attended school from Monday to Friday as predictably as night and day. We worshiped at the same church every week for years. I focused on my real estate business from morning to night—pretty orderly.

Not so much. My addiction and behaviors threw everything into disarray. I just wasn't willing to see it that way. The disarray was deep within me. I needed a new order. I needed His new order.

Prioritize Your Life's Focus: God, Spouse, Children, Business

From the time of telling Nancy about my initial adultery and later coming clean about other affairs and other addictions (everything, in fact), I went through a lot of change over a four-year period. This was from 2004 to 2007. Counseling directed some of our change, but change also came from going to meetings and Bible study, and just pondering on what I had done, who I had been, how I had been going about life, and who and what I wanted to be.

I call it my counseling and learning phase.

I was in lockdown. That's all I can call it, really. Nancy and the pastor set a number of boundaries. They controlled my phone usage. They also assigned a curfew. I had to be home every day by 3:30 no matter what was going on with my work or businesses. I accompanied this with intensive Bible study and worship.

My pastor initially instituted this after I confessed to Nancy, but she knew about Sexaholics Anonymous from her profession and said, "Go." I went. I never thought about what I had done in terms of an addiction to sex. Pastor and Nancy identified it that way for me, and I went with it. I went to S.A. meetings about twice weekly.

At the pastor's suggestion, I went to a national group event for couples presented by Family Life called Weekend to Remember. We went a week after my confession. Our pastor knew about this event. He said that we needed more help than he could give us, so why not start there? He didn't just send us there, oh no. He drove us there with his own spouse! It was in Chicago that year. Nancy and I now go yearly.

The whole experience was about how to communicate better. How to communicate at all. It also shed light on the Biblical reason for marriage and how we can best walk that out. It was the beginning of our foundation of productive conversations and moving forward together.

The CBMC, the Christian Business Men's Connection, is a men's lunch accountability and Bible study group and that helped me, too. I was close with the regional director; his wife had spoken at our church. Starting in 2009, this male accountability group helped me. I talked at church about my transgression. Everyone knew about them. No secrets were withheld.

What I learned is that God comes first.

God is to Come First

Matthew 6:31–34

> *31-32 So don't worry at all about having enough food and clothing. Why be like the heathen? For they take pride in all these things and are deeply concerned about them. But your heavenly Father already knows perfectly well that you need them,*
>
> *33 and He will give them to you if you give Him first place in your life and live as He wants you to.*
>
> *34 So don't be anxious about tomorrow. God will take care of your tomorrow too. Live one day at a time.*

"Prioritize. Put your life in order." I kept hearing this command in my quiet moments—those quiet times when the Lord God could get through to me.

I knew the church's answer. The answer was God first. God is to come first, but the real question always is, where are you spending the bulk of your time? I knew where I spent the bulk of my time. I was a workaholic. Work, work, work. Busy all the time. Doing things with my body and mind for work kept God out of my picture.

Time never lies. Tell me what you're doing with your day, and I will tell you what your "god" is. My gods were sex and money. Chasing the physical lust. Chasing my desire for more and more money as I went about growing the business at all costs.

I would lie to myself and my wife. I said I was working so hard because it was for her and for the girls, to give them a new quality of life, to build our retirement nest egg. Wrong. I was feeding my lust frenzies.

Nancy never bought that all my efforts needed to be for a higher quality of life for us. She never accepted that. That should've been a clue for me to sit down with her and come clean. To discuss a new direction with her. To put her in the role of my helpmate.

The money chasing and the hunt for sex were just ways for me to measure how well I was doing in life. Sports were absent from my life, but I had always been very competitive in life from third grade through college. I loved competitive sports, both in my small town school athletics and in college. I was a Big Eight pole vaulter and track captain. I was active in the Army ROTC, earning my officer commission.

I achieved scholarships. I was an achiever. Everything I ever did? I had to win at it, to be in first place. Second place was no place at all to me. That was my thinking as a kid and as a young man. As an older man, too, but I wasn't seeing it that way.

The chase after financial status replaced the status I sought through school sports and school achievements. Once we graduate and there're no more competitive sports, there's no way for a man to evaluate where he's going or how he's doing except through money, success, and social and economic status. That's what I told myself as I moved toward the money chase without a second thought. I subconsciously used my business success as a worldly measuring stick to tell me who I was and how I was doing at the game called life.

I was chasing money. I was chasing business success through mad growth. I was chasing social and financial status. But, whenever I failed in business, I wanted to act out. I wanted to act out sexually. I wanted either to conquer something or to see if I still "had it." Was I still attractive? Did I still have the pizzazz? I did anything to soothe my ego—to reassure myself that I was enough, that I was tops, that I was still an achiever.

Years before, when we were driving down the road, I told my wife she would have to be a single mother for a couple of years while I built my business. I felt I had given her the things she wanted in life. She had got the new house with the wooden fence. She had a dog and three children. Now it was my turn to get rewards, and it meant a bigger business. It meant proving to myself and demonstrating to others what a hotshot business success story I was. Oh, yeah—I was a CEO!

When I told her that, the shock all over her face should have been (yet another) wake-up call. Wake up and invite her in as my helpmate, my partner in life. But no, I didn't perceive that. Me, me, me! It was time to validate myself now that my wife and kids were "taken care of."

I went out and pursued my dream. I pursued it all day. Then I'd come home, go downstairs to my home office, and continue to work. I'd be on the phone nonstop, day in and day out, 24/7, weekend, week out.

It was all about business success, which meant it was all about chasing the money. It was about trying to grow something that was going to be mine. Something that I could retire on. It was all about me. Nothing about the girls or growing. Nope. It was all about my status. I, me, mine.

I wasn't able to learn what prioritizing really meant until much later—after we had gone through many memorable "Weekends to Remember." Many marriage classes. Marriage counselors. Christian counselors. It took ages before I ever began to prioritize and truly get the order of things right.

Learning and counseling. Getting my head and heart back in the right place helped God first start to come together for me. It started making sense as I built a routine for it.

A guy turned me on to KSIV 91.5 radio, which is a Christian radio station I listen to now. I gave up listening to secular music. It was all about hearing and preaching the Word. Day in and day out it was all about studying the Word. This helped me start a new routine of reserving the first part of my day for reading the Bible. I reserved the first hour after I got up each day for reading the Word and listening to Christian radio. I was in the car all day and I would be tuned to that station all the time. Making God first in this simple way is how it started.

Second Was My Spouse

To me, prioritizing Nancy second meant praying with her. I had that thought implanted in my head by my pastor.

But I could not pray with or for her at first. That was far too hard. We set a goal to pray together in the morning and evening for what she needed and what she wanted from me. I knew she mostly wanted trust and truth, to be able to trust me again, to know what I told her was the truth.

Prioritizing opened my eyes to my spouse, to Nancy.

Putting her second also came to mean date nights. I had to remember what it meant to go on a date! I remember when we first started doing it, we called it couch time or swing time. We told the kids that for dad, mom came first from now on.

I struggled at first. The kids didn't like it too much in the early days. Maybe they didn't understand the reason why anything should change. My wife always prioritized the girls, and when we started having our 20 minutes of swing time—just my wife and I connecting, focusing on each other, talking about life, and having deeper conversations—the kids felt pushed aside.

They didn't like being pushed aside, but that was the exact intention. We wanted them to feel that they did not come second, they came third in our life, and that date nights were primetime for both Mom and Dad now.

We would get away. Friday nights became our nights, and we'd have date nights out. The kids came third. God first. My spouse second. Then the kids.

Children Come Third

I adopted "Daddy Days" as a way to make the girls feel special and valued. I would take one daughter out for a date, and for three or four hours, anything she wanted to do together, that's what we did. We'd go shopping or we'd go out to eat at a restaurant. I'd open a door for her to talk with me and receive my undivided attention for a change. Each daughter got a Daddy Day.

They learned what it meant for a man-as-father to cherish them. They were really young then—8 and 10—when we started this. They later evaluated their boyfriends against the criteria I demonstrated. How I treated them was how they expected men to treat them: they expected to be prioritized in his life and respected as a woman.

When I became self-employed full time, my schedule changed and I began to take the girls to school every morning after making them lunch and doing their hair. That was the beginning of me being the father that I enjoyed being, by taking the time to love and grow my love for my children.

Eventually, I volunteered as a track coach at their elementary and junior high schools. This allowed me to meet with and understand who my daughters' friends were.

Family Life has an educational series called Passport to Purity. It involved a weekend for Nancy and me with our daughters. We discussed their commitment to virginal purity with men before marriage, behaviors with the opposite sex before marriage, and so on. Although they enjoyed the weekend, they didn't enjoy having to give their dad's business card to the young men they hoped to date!

Here is how that worked. Knowing who my daughter's friends were made it easier for me to become the one who evaluated and screened their boyfriends. The young man got my business card from my daughter, and we'd make an appointment to go out and have a meal together. The young man had to come and be interviewed by me face to face, like an application to date my daughter. My girls hated me for that. The young men experienced the trauma, too. So far, I have taken three young men to dinner. They all got that it was about setting expectations.

My daughters understood that I prioritized them, and it was for their wellbeing, safety, and for their happiness, too. Now they see that. They have developed a solid self-worth through that, and obviously, the boyfriends hated it. We haven't had too many of those situations recently because the girls understand that there's really no need for boys in their life right now and that you date in order to get married. You don't date just for something fun to do. They put that off for the years to come. They are now focused on studies and graduating from college.

Business is Fourth

I needed to put business fourth place. Not first place. Not anymore.

When my family needs me, or when God needs me, their needs come before anything I have to do with work. I know now that there are men in important job positions that stop everything they are doing at work if a child or spouse calls them on the phone. Now I get that. Family is in second and third place before business.

To acknowledge this, and not only because I was on lockdown, I reduced the hours that I worked. I committed to never exceeding forty hours a week for business, whether on job sites, at the office, or at home.

I began to take Fridays off. I'd let my employees go by noon on Fridays, too. I've since expanded this and try not to work Mondays, Fridays, or the weekend. I focus on condensing my work into Tuesdays, Wednesdays, and Thursdays—it hasn't hurt the business. But if you had told me my business would thrive under this work style, I'd never have believed you.

Business is still fourth. Is it sometimes a struggle? Does my work addiction rear its ugly head from time to time? Yes. It can get out of control when I take on a new project, coaching obligations or think of new products I want to create. Then I put it back in its place. It's dead last on my priority list now.

God first. Spouse second. Kids third. And only after them, business.

Simplify Everything

Shaun McCloskey and Steve Cook's LIFEONAIRE was a philosophy that eventually defined my new approach to life. What is the LIFEONAIRE way? Live a life—an abundant life—now. Do what you do in the world of work, but live life abundantly now.

I had to simplify my life and simplify my thinking. Once I prioritized the four most important pillars of my life, simplifying was easier.

I remembered how, I think it was Steven Covey, who said that there is a way to completely fill a jar. The jar is your life. Start with the big things—rocks. My four priorities in life were the rocks. Put them in the jar. Look at that, be with that for a while. This part may sound strange, but get in harmony with those rocks.

Only then, have a look at the extra space you may find in the jar. Put a few small pebbles in it. See how there is space for them. These are secondary priorities like a hobby, or maybe people outside the family. Notice how those pebbles have to find space around the big rocks. They cannot move the big rocks. Nope. They're not important or powerful enough to do that. The rocks come first (God, spouse, kids, business).

Then you see—ah, more space. You can pour sand into the jar. You do the same exercise. No way can the sand budge the big rocks or even the pebbles. Sand is stuff in your life that comes last; it's meaningless filler like television, video games and other mindless activities, and making more money than you need. Look at that jar closely. Hmmm… Maybe… Yes, let's pour some water in it now. NOW the jar is full. Identify the water as what it represents in your life, and get in harmony with it. Notice how it never moved the big rocks a hair.

Prioritizing helped simplify and bring balance and harmony to my life. In fact, they are probably the exact same thing…

In the beginning, I was in straight lockdown, but those restrictions helped me start getting back to simple basics—to slow down and enjoy the important things in life.

I wasn't chasing phone calls or messages at all hours anymore. I had a 40-hour week and that went for using the phone, too. If someone called outside business hours, they waited for me to be "open for business" again.

I had to be home by 3:30, and I really began to value that. Just sitting on the swing and looking at squirrels running through the backyard delighted me. Enjoying my home. A quiet thing. Formerly at that time of day, I'd have been racing around doing this or that in the business. There was such peacefulness!

When you put your life in order and prioritize things, God begins to bless you with an effortless, simple, and quiet peace. From that space, you begin to enjoy the finer things in life. This particular blessing of the Lord added no sorrow to my life, but lifted me up.

1 Timothy 6:17

> *Tell those who are rich not to be proud and not to trust in their money, which will soon be gone, but their pride and trust should be in the living God who always richly gives us all we need for our enjoyment.*

Life isn't about accumulating stuff. It's not about amassing monetary wealth. I never, ever could have said those two sentences with a straight face ten years ago. I believed these sentences after simplifying my life and clearing the clutter as opposed to accumulating and chasing after more.

Life's beauty and bounty is about relationships with the Lord, with your spouse, with your children, and with others who have entered your life. I began to understand and value that. I began to want and seek it. I remade my life, built around these new priorities.

CHAPTER SIX

My Spouse Speaks

This chapter is for Nancy to speak. She is my spouse, my help-mate, my partner, and my support through highs and lows. The mother of our three most beautiful and delightful children. The one who—against all odds and her own grief and pain—stayed with me. She made me a better husband, a better man.

For all those years that I neglected to acknowledge her pain—the pains of who I was, the pains of my physical and emotional absences, the devastation created through my transgressions and my behaviors—I ask, repeatedly, for her forgiveness.

I love you Nancy.

Nancy Speaks: A Hole in My Heart

It was a fall day in September 2003. I drove home from work to let the dog out, get the mail, and then go and pick up the girls from school. As I opened the garage door for the dog, white light suddenly blinded me. I could not see. I started to crawl outside on the driveway and, thankfully, my sight returned, but I felt very weak and my head pounded. This marked the start of the most tragic year of my life.

What was that all about? I had a stroke at 39 years of age. I was healthy, in good shape, no health concerns. Why did this happen?

After several trips to the emergency room, numerous MRIs and ECGs showed that I had a hole in my heart. I required surgery. They told me that the surgery was fairly simple—no open-heart surgery. The surgeon entered through the femoral artery in my leg, the main artery, and put an umbrella-type patch in my heart.

The surgery went well, but I started experiencing panic and anxiety attacks for the first time. I felt like I was going to die.

This was a lie. Several months later in January 2004, my mother fell ill and went into the hospital. She fell into a coma and eventually moved into a nursing home. In March, she was in hospice, and my family was waiting for her to die. We sat in the nursing home when my husband started acting strange.

I asked him what was wrong. It was a Sunday, and we had just come from church. It was communion Sunday, but Tim refused to take communion, and went to the altar to pray. I asked him at the nursing home what was wrong.

We went outside to talk, and he proceeded to tell me very calmly that he was having an affair.

I started to cry and get upset. I yelled. I tried to figure out what was going on, but I eventually told him to just go home and take the girls with him.

This was the next stage of fighting for my life, and the fear of what would happen—it wasn't just about fighting for my body's health anymore. It wasn't about helping my mom through her last days, either, or my grief with that. But it was all of that, and more now. The fight for my marriage with Tim piled on top.

My mother died three days later, and I was numb. I could not eat. I could barely think. I felt depressed and angry all at the same time. What was I going to do? I had faith, but this was a big job.

I told Tim we were going to see the pastor and talk to him the next day, and that Monday we did. This led to many long nights, many fights, and the realization of who my husband really was. It felt like living through a bad version of Sleeping with the Enemy, I thought.

One night after driving, and not long after the nursing home confession, Tim parked and told me the whole story of his past. He spoke about past abuse, about a pornography addiction, about affairs, and more. It all just heaped on me at once. I sat in silence. I wanted to run out of the van and get away from this man. Who was he? He was not the man I married.

I wanted to run. Instead, a very loud voice coming from God came into my head and said, "Help him. Help him."

My first reaction was, "Oh no, God. You must be wrong. I can't do this."

"Help him," God said again in my head, very loudly.

I thought, "I don't know what to do, God."

"Help him," was the reply again.

I stayed.

We went to many counseling sessions. Tim attended Sexaholics Anonymous groups. We researched sex addictions in detail. We needed real information.

We threw out the pornographic tapes he had hidden in the house. We put blockers on the computers; we set up rules and restrictions on him that the pastor helped us put in place. Tim couldn't be alone with women. He had a curfew, a time he had to be home every day no matter what. We had full viewing of his phone calls and Internet activities.

This is crazy, I thought. "I can't do this," I repeated to myself.

I tried to get help for myself, too. I went to S-Anon (support) groups. I found two other Christian women dealing with the same thing from their husbands. One was divorced and one was still married. We met regularly to help one another. It was good advice that I got from these women, but it was still very hard.

It was so hard. I would never want any woman to feel this kind of pain. I felt this kind of pain for years, and I thought I could not handle this. I thought I had to deal with all of Tim's up and downs, his moods, and his irrational patterns of thinking.

The whole double-mindedness was enough to drive a wife crazy. "Who am I talking to today?" I'd ask myself. The good Tim or the bad Tim? The honest Tim or the liar? What am I hearing today out of his mouth? The truth or a smooth lie? His sneaky behavior, his lies—it was all so much to unravel.

We kept a bargain that he had to have an "empty bucket." It meant if Tim did something wrong and slid backwards—if he watched porn, or masturbated, or called a woman from the past—he had to empty his bucket by confessing it to me. This is a very hard thing for a woman to hear her husband confess when she thinks everything is okay.

But this was the start of helping him be accountable. He eventually had to have a male Christian accountability partner to talk to as well. A wife should not be her husband's only accountability partner, because it's much too hard. He also needs a neutral person, and he found one that helped.

Through many years, God kept our marriage together. God kept it together. God kept me together in myself when I thought I would surely fall apart. God got us through this time.

It was not easy, and the world and other women would tell me to leave Tim. Divorce him. Pack up the girls and leave, but I chose to follow what God told me. He said, "Help him. Forgive him. I am going to use him." So I did the best I could: I followed God.

God told me all these things. I have been blessed by staying with my husband rather than leaving him. We have a strong, open, honest marriage now. Our relationship with God is stronger than ever.

Our children have seen what God can do. Being obedient and serving the Lord always reaps more blessings than doing what the world says. Our children see that. Tim and I see that. I thank God for all he has done and that he continues to do.

CHAPTER SEVEN

———

Becoming a Man-Husband-Father

Submit to the Ways of the Word, Not to the Ways of the World

I don't think that all people who succumb to the ways of the world act from addiction, but I think many of them—I should say, many of us—act from an emptiness. Addictions and routines are only an attempt to feel filled up, to feel fulfilled, to imagine that we are doing everything we can to live up to our potential.

Manhood

I went through a phase where I read lots and lots and lots and lots of books. The Bible was primary among all the books on spiritual growth, personal growth, and guidance that I read.

I have read a lot on my path to becoming who, how, and what the Lord needs me to be. I'm now on my path back to putting

God first, which is what a real man needs to do. I'm on my path to becoming the vessel He needs me to be—to being the man, husband, and father my family needs me to be. I'm sorting out my priorities before myself and God and making them daily realities.

The most critical book of all for me was The Power of a Praying Husband by Stormie Omartian. It helped establish a healthy foundation of prayer in my life.

I first started reading that book because our pastor told us to pray together. When I prayed with my wife the first time, I could not do it. I felt so angry and so upset, and she didn't understand why. She could pray with me, but I could not pray with her … or for her.

Where did all that anger come from? Maybe from my perception of Nancy's abandonment of our early shared business life, when she chose the children over me. Wherever it came from, I had to deal with it, because there is one thing I learned: it's impossible to pray in any sincere manner for a person when you're angry with them.

I would pray improperly. When I first got that book, I would go through it and pick all the things out that I wanted my wife to change in herself. (Yes, you are reading that correctly: she had to change. Oh, boy.)

I'd pray for those changes in her, and I'd say, "God, please change this woman so that she can be the woman that I want." (Yes, you are reading that correctly: The woman I want. Oh, boy.)

Being the selfish, arrogant person that I was—and could not see that I was—I would pray that way over and over and over.

I don't know what happened, but our pastor realized what I was doing. He nailed me. He said, "You know, that's not the way to pray for your spouse." What he said is, "You pray for your spouse, for the wonderful blessings of God that he has for her, and to make her all that she is supposed to be—all that God desires for her to be."

That was a totally new way of praying for my wife. It wasn't about me! Oh, boy.

So I got with the prayer program and started openly praying. "God, you create in this woman what you want her to be, and help make the adjustments in me to accept that."

I had to change. Wow. The idea transformed me. Ha, so I say now, but … wait for it!

Here is what my new thinking became: "Now I have to change? Now I'm giving up everything. I'm making all the changes. I am the one doing all the changing. My wife gets off free. She doesn't have to do anything."

That was how I twisted it all up, and it frustrated me for some years! I thought, I'm just openly praying for God to make this woman whatever he wants her to be, and I've got to do all the changing?

Whoever said prayer was easy wasn't getting through to me yet. That is an understatement. Selfish me.

It took a while to get used to it … and to understand it. Slowly each day, I opened the prayer book and selected the topic I thought my wife would need the most help in for that day. Did I say arrogant? But, I was also blind …

It was a big step for me not to be selfish, and it took many years because I was not seeing any change happening in our life. She didn't have to change, according to the guidance I received, and it frustrated me. We began to pray together morning and night, ever so slowly.

Later God revealed to me that Nancy was farther along in her journey than I thought she was. She focused on the things with God that she needed to focus on. And maybe, He would deal with her at a time, and when that time came, she would work on her own stuff, not mine.

Counseling educated both of us. I couldn't do the work for my wife, and my wife couldn't do the work for me.

We were both responsible for our own work.

Husbandhood

Sometime later, the Lord led me to take Nancy on a trip to Colorado Springs. We had no idea why we were to go. The Lord just said, "Go." My wife believed enough in me at that time, and we spent the money. We flew out to Colorado Springs, rented a car, and we just drove. A day or two into this, we drove to the Air Force Academy.

On the way back from the Air Force Academy, we noticed this building on the side of the road, and we pulled off there. We soon realized that it was the Focus on the Family campus. We stayed there, we went to the bookstore, and we just took a tour. We just investigated it, thoroughly excited. You see, at home, as we were listening to KSIV 91.5, Focus on the Family was a regularly scheduled program that came on the radio. We knew what its impact was. We just had a huge passion for that ministry.

We met some friends who were involved in real estate in the past from St. Louis. They owned a motel and were out there enjoying their life. We went on from there for a drive to Pikes Peak into the mountains and just walked around.

I need to backtrack a bit about where Nancy and I were at around the time of this trip.

I had told Nancy about my adultery in March 2004. In September 2003, Nancy had a stroke. She'd fallen in the garage, and neighbors helped and called me. On top of the challenge of her stroke and recovering from it, within three days of me confessing to her in April 2004, her mom died from meningitis.

I remembered the time when my wife suffered a stroke. She was in her 30s, and it was a huge shock. She lost weight due to the stroke and thought she looked great and wonderful at a size zero or a size two. I remember a picture we took, way up in the mountain where she was standing against this cabin. After her stroke, she lost a tremendous amount of weight. She liked having lost it. I did not. I was like, "Man, my wife is so skinny." That was a time where I once again had to pull back and be with her.

When I shared my darkest secret of adultery, it was at the worst time in her life. Talk about selfish. I selfishly ignored the bad timing for Nancy. The timing was all about me, but the stress was all on Nancy.

Her mother was on her deathbed and died just three days after my confession, and she had just suffered that stroke and wasn't fully recovered in all the ways necessary to get well again. She had a hole in her heart, and she had a surgical repair. This dreadful personal time for her was a time that she could still have faith in me and say, "This is what the Lord has told me to do."

So there we were in Colorado. We found ourselves out in the mountains at its highest peak possible, wondering what God had for us. We didn't know and we went to church later that week.

We were homebound to St. Louis. On the return trip, we were walking around the airport. I recognized a woman who was walking beside us and talking. She had blond hair. I kept thinking, "This woman looks familiar for some reason." I could not put my finger on it.

As Nancy and I spoke, we sat at the same gate as this woman, and I kept looking at her. I got out the book I was reading on the plane when I happened to flip over to the back cover. I recognized that the woman sitting across from me was its author, Stormie Omartian! That was why she looked so familiar. The book was, of course, The Power of the Praying Husband.

I got up and went and talked to her, and told her the problems my wife and I had. I asked her if she would sign my book and chatted about how great the book was and how transformational it had been in my life. I told her that my daughter had said, "Man, wouldn't it be nice if there was a book for children?"

Stormie said, "Well, you wouldn't believe this, but I do have that in my schedule of things to do! But we're in the midst of a move, and, well, I got it started but, you know, it isn't out yet. Have your daughter contact me, and maybe she'll get to write a piece in the book." She said she had been at Focus on the Family preparing for the National Day of Prayer.

We did that. We followed up with her when we got back home, and my daughter Kayla contacted her and gave her an idea of something she would like to see in the book. Stormie graciously let her have a piece, a summary quote as I recall, in her book for children called The Power of a Praying Child.

We don't know what was yet to come from the trip, but we got to meet Stormie Omartian, who inspired both my wife and myself. My wife and I have read those books to shreds. My wife has taken hers apart and put it in a binder; my copy is tattered and worn out, and pages have come loose, so between our two copies, we've worn those books out.

It's helped me be a better man, a better husband, and a better father.

As I practiced being a better man, I learned to surrender 100% of myself to God, to be obedient to God, to be consecrated and set apart for God, to be focused, and to be ready to move at any moment's notice when He tells me to be ready to move. To be humble. To fear God. To hear God. To be trustworthy. To be willing and open to God.

No coincidence that this hearkens back to "Put God First."

As a husband, I've learned to be adultery free. I am being delivered from the compulsion of those addictive, compulsive activities that used to control me. Do not think for a moment that Satan doesn't try daily to reclaim me for his army!

I progressively gain recovery from the faults that are burned into my mind, the battles that I struggle with at night. The battle is on—daily.

I've learned to love my wife. I've learned to communicate better with Nancy. I've learned that I must die for my wife and to myself and that she is to become my best friend. We're working toward that right now. Together.

Fatherhood

I've learned to become a better father. I told my children what I had done, the hidden sin in my life. Twenty minutes after confessing my infidelity to my wife, I went to my kids and told them, too. They were so young. Probably not the best thing to do in hindsight … This was a process of dumping on my kids. A way of coming clean from my sin. It was not the appropriate thing to do, especially at their young ages.

As a result, and from the very beginning, my children knew why and what we were battling. We never kept it a secret from them. With that, we've had open communication with our kids. From their own hindsight, they have said they wouldn't change a thing today. It's made us a stronger family. We are the family that we are today because of the battles that we've fought and won together.

This is as strong as our family has ever been. I'd die for my kids. We've had many teaching moments. Kayla once wrote a school paper about what was happening in our family. It was entitled, "The Worst Day of My Life." We sat on the kitchen floor. We cried and discussed the paper and the trauma it had created for her at that moment in time. That was one of the lowest days of my life.

Whenever things would come up, we would take that moment to teach our kids. We laugh together now; we have ridiculous laughing moments. We travel together. We've created memories that are beyond jokingly funny.

We talk about having a family channel and a TV show, and we've joked about that for years. That's a whole new book in itself, but talking about it drew us closer and closer together as a family.

I have learned that we are not friends to, but the parents of, our children. I spoke in a sermon on Father's Day not long ago about the seven things a father wants for his children. That came from my heart, the heart my children fill. Here are the seven things I discussed with my congregation that a father wants for his children, and what I wish for my own children:

1. Safety. We strive to keep you safe in your younger years in the world as you learn how people and the world work. We keep you safe in our shared home.

2. Eat well. We strive as breadwinners and priest of the house to provide the nourishment from food for your bodies as we guide you in how to be spiritually nourished by the Word.

3. Grow up right. We strive to be the best role model, mentor and guide that we can be; and when we get it wrong, we don't cover up but admit it and move back onto the right path. To His Path. Together.

4. Grow into maturity. We want to be there for you, but know (and it is so hard!) that we eventually have to let you go to learn your own lessons and make your own way. Helping you into adulthood from teen, to young adult still in school, to full adult out in the world, to letting you do it all your own way, is our job. We call this "adulting" in our household.

5. Get married to a perfect helpmate. I want you to know you have found the right one like I did when I saw Nancy. I remember telling someone back then about Nancy, "I saw the halo and, whoop, there she is! There's the one I'll marry!"

6. Know always how to get home. We strive to keep our home a safe haven to which you can always return, anytime. This is the earthly home of our family. We strive to show you the path to (and back to) the Lord when you have lost your way home to Him.

7. Prayers for my kids are heard and answered. We believe, and constantly remind ourselves as fathers, that the Lord hears you, listens to you, and that you are listening for His answers when they come. Because they do.

CHAPTER EIGHT

———

Abandon Your Dreams— God's Will, Not Tim's Will

Learning to Let Thy Will Be Done

I still wanted to run a real estate company. In the world of business, real estate was my passion. I wanted to accumulate rental properties for passive income, and I had gone into long-term debt to do so.

I did want to listen to, hear and follow the Lord's guidance for me. I knew it was the only way to pull myself out of my sexual acting out and to rebuild my family and establish confidence in me. To do that, I had to change my thinking about a whole lot of things.

Here are some of the incidents and events that helped me stay on the Lord's Path to my healing and my new mission.

Letting Go of Dreams

My dream had been to make enough money from real estate to retire and live well with Nancy. To give the kids everything they needed from us for a good start in life. Abandoning real estate, no longer using debt financing, no longer going into business debt—that was hard. No longer working like a crazy man, as a slave to the money—that was also a hard habit and perspective to change.

Abandoning my business goals and dreams of wealth to follow the Lord's command was hard for me to do, I will never deny it. It was confusing more times than I can count. I thought that I had surrendered 100% of my life to God, but He kept saying, "Do not that work (not real estate), but full time ministry in church—you don't need the security of the business and income."

I needed to put a lot of faith in the Lord and in His direction for me to trust that my path would become clear. It was, as I look back, a winding path.

What did I give up? My eight companies had lots of emotion wound up in them, and lots of personal pride. I needed to close out all of them and be free of that aspect of my past mistakes. I did that. I sold it all or otherwise let it go. I started all over from scratch, in the ways and at the times I was guided by the Lord.

When I went to close it all down, I remembered the several years we were MBE-certified (Minority Business Enterprise), and how it had taken months to get that certification. It's extremely difficult to get the MBE certification. That I would truly have to abandon this dream? That was the Lord's Vision for me. And so, I abandoned that dream as the Lord guided me to do.

I had closed down all of the businesses related to Rhino Homes and KJR Industries, which dealt with all of what I call the dirty years of my life—when I was growing the business and when I was deep in sexual sin. That was easy to do because I knew that it was all soiled, tainted. God wasn't going to bless anything that came out of that.

I ended up closing down numerous companies—five or six LLCs and everything related to them. I had given away all the business equipment, and didn't take anything from the old business to the new location, just so it wouldn't contaminate the new vision, so to speak. The old Tim had contaminated those businesses by blocking the Lord and His Word.

I think of how Luke said it in Chapter 9:23–25.

23 Then He said to them all: "Whoever wants to be my disciple must deny themselves and take up their cross daily and follow me.

24 For whoever wants to save their life will lose it, but whoever loses their life for me will save it.

25 What good is it for someone to gain the whole world, and yet lose or forfeit their very self?"

The Lord did not prohibit me from business per se. I was clear on that. I needed to go about business and money making in a radically different way, however.

Blessings to Others

Blessings to Others demonstrates to me that the Lord doesn't work on the human clock or calendar. This unfolded over so many years that I couldn't be sure where the Lord was leading me with this new ministry. It required quite a lot of patience to stick with it.

I started a non-profit that we named Blessings to Others (BTO) because the Lord had spoken to me and given me that name in the summer of 2003. Later in the fall of that year, I filed as a state non-profit.

Here is how I came think of a way to get initial funding for the BTO mission: The Lord tells us we should set aside money so that when Jesus or an apostle comes into town, we would not have to take up an offering.

1 Corinthians 16:2

On the first day of every week, each one of you should set aside a sum of money in keeping with your income, saving it up, so that when I come no collections will have to be made.

In the beginning, the employees who were making more and were willing to give to the fund donated funds to help other employees who had a need. It didn't all materialize right away, though. When we first started out, we instead used Blessings to Others to help employees who needed assistance with utility bills and the like.

Later in 2005, following Hurricane Katrina, I opened up some of my rentals to be used as housing for the people that had moved to St. Louis and needed assistance. After that time had passed, BTO slowed down, and nothing new was done with it until January 2011 when a friend of mine came to me about creating housing for the homeless.

Following a fast in June of 2011, I found myself standing in the midst of the Edward Jones Dome in St. Louis at that time, and God birthed an impression within me of "10,000 free and clear homes in ten years." He had said to me that we'd receive 10,000 houses needed by people who'd experienced a setback. They'd be free and clear homes.

We submitted our initial paperwork to the IRS for non-profit approval in the summer of 2012.

We later developed a program to provide twelve weeks of Christian life skills to people benefiting from the homes. This new vision of Blessings to Others took years to unfold for us.

We went through some complicated hoops to clearly separate BTO from our commercial businesses so that the federal authorities could give us our Letter of Determination as a non-profit corporation. We got that confirmation for Blessings to Others from the IRS in December 2013, ten years after the vision first came to me. It is a now a non-profit entity taking a message about God to others from the platform of real estate and spiritual life education.

It's truly what God meant when he told me to abandon all my dreams and former worldly goals. You have to guide yourself daily and take up your cross, as Luke says to do. He talks about surrendering yourself to the Lord daily.

Putting Out My Fleece

In the process of putting myself on the Lord's path and staying on it, I came across a way to put myself to the test of trust in the Lord. I became skeptical at times, believe me. I didn't trust myself, much less the non-traditional ways of God. But He brought validation to me that He was my Way and my Light.

I had become acquainted with a dear friend of CBMC (Christian Business Men's Connection). His wife was strong in prayer and had come to give a presentation at our church. He had put out a fleece (this is "asking the Lord for a sign"), and I remember him telling me about it. I had never put out a fleece. I had never asked the Lord to send me a sign. That dear friend told me, "Tim, the one thing I can tell you, if you put out a fleece, you have to do what God tells you to do. You cannot not do it when he answers it."

I put the fleece out, and it came back confirming Blessings to Others. I was like Biblical Gideon at that point, and I thought, "Well, surely, but I need another sign." I was working and earning an income then, but there was no income from BTO and it was still very much a walk of faith.

Another friend from church told me she'd had a dream about me and "two signs above the door" of my office. I'd been contemplating putting two signs up on my building: one for my for-profit business and the other one for the nonprofit business. She said, "I saw a vision, and it was Blessings to Others." Now, I had never given her the name I was considering, but it had appeared in her dream: Blessings to Others. She confirmed what I needed to be doing. That was the confirming sign I'd asked for. From that moment on, I started working and focusing more of my time towards Blessings to Others. I had put out a fleece and now had to do what it guided me to do.

Renewed Connections

In the process of putting myself on the Lord's path and trusting it would lead where I needed to go, being in touch with my network of Christian friends and associates always happened when it benefited all of us. Renewed connections with friends brought more validation to the path I was taking. Here are two examples.

Some years earlier, my friend Steve Cook had been given the word LIFEONAIRE and was trying to develop what that meant (more than a millionaire—more than a person with lots of money; a truly abundant person, an alive individual, and blessed in many areas). We spoke together about a book that he wanted to publish about the concept he had been given. It was going through several different rewrites and idea shifts.

I left Steve to his book writing, and about three years later reconnected by phone with him. By then, we had the letter from the IRS that made Blessings to Others a bona fide nonprofit, tax-exempt organization. By then, LIFEONAIRE was close to publication, ultimately getting a very successful response.

When I was on Day 19 of another 21-day fast, I got back in touch with Steve. He said he was building houses in Guatemala (his mission ministry) and might need a 501(c)3 to raise funds. We thought of BTO.

I later called another friend of Steve's and mine, Shaun McCloskey, Co-Author of LIFEONAIRE. He wanted me to share my testimony with his REIA (Real Estate Investment Association group) that he'd be purchasing and starting in a couple months' time. This was in February 2014—ten years since I dropped out of the real estate scene. Now here I was, being invited back. Later he asked me to present a class in "controlling your contractor." To my surprise, he moved the REIA location to the exact place that, ten years prior, ended my real estate career.

My wife would be in the audience for support, a flashback point for both of us. Quite an emotional evening!

Unpredictable

None of what I did to divest myself of businesses, to heal my addictions, and to rebuild my life with my wife and children and with the Lord, happened in a clear plan of first A, then B, and finally C. I cannot say that any of it was predictable. I could tell you the long, complicated chronology and each action I took to follow the Lord's guidance on this. Just know that each new lesson I was taught, and each new action I was directed to take, happened when it needed to.

I was called into ministry while still in the process of shutting down the eight companies. My companies were my income, so my income was gone. Scary for a guy with three kids! I didn't know how I'd make money for my family when I quit real estate. I had volunteered to lead my church because the Lord told me, "Volunteer and the money will come." A leap of faith for a guy who had transgressed the Lord's Word and the Lord's Way for so many years. Later, after some volunteering, the church did decide it could pay me $2,000/month. Then Blessings to Others emerged as part of my ministry as a nonprofit 501(c)3 organization, helping others as I have described elsewhere. I took a leap of trust in the Lord when He said the words, "10,000 homes"— for a real estate guy that was beyond huge!

I had a particular fear of having too little income. It went against all my dreams and goals of wealth. That shook me up, but I stayed the course and held on to my faith in the Lord's guidance.

In the end, Headache-Free Properties came to me as a means to earn some additional income. Yes. After dissolving the other real estate-related companies, I created this new real estate company. Why? How is this different?

I live my faith through the business, as a Christian businessman. I follow the Lord's directive to avoid debt. I run the business in a few hours a week; no longer caught up in a job for all my waking hours. With Headache-Free Properties, I show Christian real estate entrepreneurs how to create passive, no debt income by partnering with other Christian individuals looking to get a return on their financial investment. One party creates a real estate opportunity; the other co-invests his extra cash with him. No indebtedness. I love the coaching and the guidance I can give other Christians thanks to my years of experience in real estate. I have an easier workday, with more balance.

Not A, then B, then C, not by any means. My way back to God was not a logical progression of events or steps. Nonetheless, it all makes sense to me now. This is how my trust and faith in God as my provider materialized for my family and me.

More unpredictability lies in how money comes to Nancy and me when it is needed. It is still amazing to me that Nancy and I have been able to cover the gap financially for our three girls, who are in college, and have a combined annual tuition of almost $100,000. Thank goodness they have excelled in school and receive several scholarships and grants. But God has been amazing every school year with His timing. Income provided matches income needed—never early but never late. I don't know how we manage that, but we do. And we manage to live well, with everything we need. I took those leaps of faith with Nancy by my side and was blessed by the Lord. He provided. He provides for us and blesses us every day. Faith is believing in what the Lord has promised and moving on His instruction before you see the promise materialize.

CHAPTER NINE

———

Reproduce One First, Before Many

Teach the Cycle

This chapter is about my passion for helping others and my search to apply biblical concepts to everyday life. You first have to understand how to help one person change his life before you can develop and administer a program to help many individuals make changes.

After years of struggling to understand what my purpose in life was, God made it quite clear that my mission is to help people apply biblical concepts to their everyday lives, not just on Sunday, not just on Wednesday, but every day of their lives. We're supposed to walk and act as Jesus did, and He helped people all His waking hours.

He helped me understand my passion to help other people in breathing into their lives. I call it pouring into someone's life. There were several people that I tried to help (I have changed their names to protect their privacy). The ones that come to mind are Tony Arrons, Bobby Basket, and Matt Fish. These were all people that I wanted to pour myself into, people who I would help.

I made a minimum six-month commitment to them and poured into their lives. Day in and day out we worked together. I'd call them, we'd get together, and we'd read and study the Bible. I tried to get them to memorize verses, but people have to want this more for themselves than I want it for them.

I worked with Tony Arrons. He was a foster kid, a part of the system his whole childhood. He was "my project." Arrons stayed in my house from time to time. Now he's in California, doing well.

I worked with Bobby, a homeless man. His wife had lost him, literally—and we found him in a deserted garage. He started attending our church. He lived in a Blessings to Others house.

I worked with Matt Fish. He came to the church for help on his own. He wanted to work; he was a recovering heroin addict.

The Assignment was "Discipleship and Service to Community." It was not about my ego. It was about "Can I give them what they need when they are ready for it, by me being His vessel?"

You see, I often wanted to provide this service more than they wanted to receive it. I would get frustrated, and I would pour myself into their life, and sometimes, I would almost sacrifice the love of my children for this work and the mission of helping other people. I often had to back off the mission sometimes.

I found that people have to want to change—just like me. I had to want the change before the tools came to me. People need to know a process and have a process to change. I myself had to know that. They had to know who was able to make them change. We can't make others change because they dig in or stay blind to a glaring problem that you see but they do not. We can't even make ourselves change until we surrender. We have to surrender and submit ourselves to the Lord and to have Him change us.

Others had to be in the place that I finally got to. I had to be open and willing to change myself and do the work involved to make the changes.

I found this to be true of everyone else also. One has to be willing to do the work necessary to change, and then it's a continual process. It's not just a matter of, "I'm going to try this for a while, and then I'll go do this other thing and come back to this project later and try some more." It's a daily commitment that you make to the Lord's work, to making yourself His.

There's no testimony without the test. That means, there is going to be a test, and with that test, often comes the re-test. I used to joke with a friend that I find myself revisiting the same point again and again, and I get tired of taking the re-test.

Then God says, "This is really simple. Just learn the principle I'm trying to teach you, and then you don't have to take the re-test."

I now know that if I want to avoid the re-test, I need to ask the Lord what principle do I have to learn. Then, the Lord would ask me, "Do you want to be a world changer?" When God gives you a God-sized assignment, God will give you a vision, and He will also provide for you. He'll give you provision for that. He'll lead you to what you need and bring you what is needed for you to complete the assignment.

During that timeframe, it may seem it is going to be a much larger task or goal than you can handle on your own. You have to be patient and you have to clean your life up. You have to observe what the Lord is showing you. You have to arrive for work, and you have to get it done as it is given to you.

Most importantly, there's no whining. God doesn't like whining, so don't whine. Whining is just you, in your little body and your little mind, trying to tell the Lord that you don't trust Him to guide you through a larger task in ways allowing you to achieve the final outcome. Trust in the Lord.

Proverbs 3:5–6

⁵ Trust in the LORD with all your heart and lean not on your own understanding;

⁶ in all your ways submit to him, and he will make your paths straight.

Learn to Teach One First

You have to learn to duplicate yourself. You have to have a proven, repeatable, simple system for people to follow.

Christians need to learn how to create a residual cash flow. How not to be B.U.S.Y. (Being Under Satan's Yoke). That's busy-work, not the Lord's work. That's an old human pattern that we got into when we looked away from the Lord's guidance.

Being under Satan's yoke is slavery. Slavery is also, "I have to work hard so that in 35 years I will have something." Now is the thing; in 35 years is not the thing. Being in Today, in Now. It is what the book LIFEONAIRE is all about.

We have to get out of the bondage of financial slavery. When we accept that the Bible holds the answer to every question that we're going to have today, we can find our answer. We have to study it and we have to work, but every answer is right there in the Book.

CHAPTER TEN

———

Speak and Influence Others

Your Own Amazing Life

After I had learned how to talk to and help one person with some confidence, I was ready to talk to more than one person at a time. To do so, I now use what is called the Amazing Life Process with people.

The Process deals with a three-fold problem shared by most of us:

- We are pushed to be busy all the time, believing that our schedule needs to be filled with activity from morning till night.

- We are encouraged by a variety of outside pressures to be in debt—for our homes, our stuff, our education, and so on.

- We float along without direction.

The Amazing Life Process develops a consistent way of approaching your life each and every day. Your Amazing Life encompasses faith, family and finances. It is the walk we take every day that incorporates all three of those and that is found in the Word of God. The Word constantly instructs us and gives us the answers for everything that we will face in life. If we will only go to the Word and begin to study it and to see the patterns that He has laid out from the Old Testament to the New Testament, we can see that He is a God of love, who instructs us daily to walk according to His ways. Not that He is such a hard taskmaster, but there are laws of the universe to follow. When we follow them, our lives are benefited. Not just our individual lives, but our family's lives and the lives of all those that come in contact with us.

This has been a journey that I've been on for ten years. I was a nominal Christian, one who did the religious acts ever since I was a child when my mom would take me to church. Nevertheless, it wasn't until I was hard pressed with a life crisis that I'd turn to the Lord for help. When I was at my most broken point, He reached out to me and showed me His love. In that love, He began to mentor me and walk me constantly through situations where I was given the choice to obey or disobey, and when I chose to obey, I learned. I grew in the aspects of how to live life. The faith aspect took me from being an outside individual layperson, who then began to study to be ordained as a pastor. This took six years of taking two classes a year, but I was moved to do so.

At the end of that time, I was to lead a small community church that the pastor left and turned over to me. I believe in that training period God was using that as a moment to speak to me on what it took to teach, show, grow and prepare a group of people (including me) for how to walk through life using His word. Much frustration came out of that, and I believed He released me in June of 2015 and said, "That's been the training ground for you, but now the mission is to take the private pulpit to the public." That has been my assignment. An Amazing Life is all about following His word and applying it.

One of the things that we have noticed is the family. The situation that caused me to sink to such depth is I thought I was honestly going to lose my wife and kids because of a sexual sin that I had committed. Through this time period, God spoke to my wife and me. Yes, we had a problem that was a scar in our marriage, but we were promised if we worked towards healing it, it would be like a weld mark between two pieces of metal, and that's exactly what came to be. We have a marriage stronger than we ever had before. Through that, our children noticed and walked along the same path with us.

We were able to share with them as we grew. They experienced our ups and downs, no doubt. They, too, began to carve out a salvation for themselves that they fought for, and they had to struggle through and understand. They had to get the true meaning of salvation and how we are sanctified through the Lord, who is always teaching us and showing us the way.

We have a family unit that is stronger than most I believe. Many of our children's friends have recognized what we have. We're the house on the block where everybody comes to. It's been God that we have glorified, and there's not anything special that we have done unless it is following the Lord's Commands. We just try to live according to what He told us to do. As a result, we have a family unit that is trusting, loving, and interdependent upon one another, as we all depend upon the Lord.

I have become the priest of the house. I, at one time, did not fully value my wife or my children. I only was chasing money. I wanted to create this empire that was bigger than anything else, where I could grade myself according to how much money I had accumulated. I know people do that today. They're chasing, always chasing. They're always proud of how busy they are.

B.U.S.Y. That acronym stands for Being Under Satan's Yoke, B.U.S.Y. So many people are so proud to say, "I'm busy, busy, busy!" Well, let me tell you, the Lord does not want us busy. The Lord wants us available. To hear, to trust, to share His way and His Word.

I believe that we as Christians today cannot listen and understand what our purpose is in life until we solve the money thing. With a money solution, we have peace and time to spend with our family, to listen and be attentive to the Lord, what He directs us to do, and how to do it. There is a lifestyle the Lord prescribes for us to live in, and part of that is the Sabbath. The Sabbath day, the day of rest, was created and given to Adam, but Adam gave it away, and we have been chasing around and trying to make the soil produce for us ever since, so to speak.

In doing this chasing after a livelihood and money, it has strained our relationship with the Lord. It isn't until we get that under control and create passive income for our needs that we can truly give focused attention to the Lord.

Now, am I saying that we have to have everything in place before we work for the Lord? Did I? No! I certainly did not follow what would appear to be any rational or logical progression of events to get where I am now! No, because any time God gives us an assignment, He's going to make a way for us to complete it. That is part of the walk of faith that we have to take as well, even if it seems like a leap of faith. There are some worldly things that we should be putting in place that are separate from the Kingdom life so that both aspects of life will help us be all we can be in the Lord's eyes.

In the Amazing Life Process, we help you apply those aspects of the Word that should be put into place in our worldly life. There are Six Pillars to our program, and it may take 12–48 months to fully embrace and work through the entire process and be fully transformed.

Here are the 6 Pillars we help you put in place:

1. Create your life plan. What do you want out of life? Are you willing to map out goals for the next year? How about 5, 10, 20 years and beyond, and work toward it?

2. Determine which business you might find success in. Which business ideas can you list for your family that match your passions and gifts?

3. Create a business leveraged with the Internet that will allow you to generate 40 hours of income on 15 hours of oversight. Think in terms of residual or passive income from your endeavors.

4. Identify and overcome the blind spots in your life preventing you from being successful in life and business. This is moving into more and more freedom from personal bondage, whether spiritual, emotional, physical or mental.

5. Determine your purpose in life. What is your passion? What do you yearn for that you believe will fulfill you and give you direction?

6. Find your God assignment and follow the lead of the Lord. Accept God's assignment for you, in the world or behind the scenes. Change the world; take dominion.

We are hoping to create a family that encompasses and is connected with the community that it lives in—a family that makes an impact on both its local and global community.

When we begin to take dominion over the kingdom that we have here (our worldly life), we eclipse the darkness with the light. That is our mission—making more and more disciples, who are followers and students of Christ. Who are seen and perceived by others to have something greater than what they have.

The challenge of the Church today is that "we" (Christians) don't look any different in worldly terms than "they" (non-Christians) do. It's only when we look different than they do and start commanding things to be as the Lord says "on Earth as it is Heaven" then those that wish to have a more purposeful life can say "I want to follow Christ, too. I want what they have."

I believe it begins with the desire, stating a well-determined, clear intention to live a life different from the one now unfolding for you. You don't have to live the life you're living now. You can live an Amazing Life. We're glad to show you how to do that: www.AmazingLife-Now.com

Boldness

I believe we need to be bolder Christians. We have to speak up today. We can't be a silent majority. We're losing ground to bold non-Christians every single day. We are drawn relentlessly into the struggles and hatreds of the world. We have to be bold as we stand on the Rock of the Lord Jesus Christ. We have to know the way as well as show the way. We have to be an example for what the Lord is doing in our life—as a demonstration of His power in all lives. When we are living An Amazing Life every day, then we give people not only our example, we give them hope and a Path. We spread the Light and overcome the Darkness.

Speak and Influence Others

This is where I find myself in the present day. I feel that the Lord wants to use me to speak to thousands upon thousands of people. It's the next chapter in my life. Our girls are attending college. One thing I do know is that I get my greatest teammate back, and she is my wife. We are empty nesters now. Nancy will be retiring soon from 25+ years as a school social worker. We will start a new ministry together.

When we first started out, we were known as Tim and Nancy, Tim and Nancy. Everywhere we went, everyone called us Tim and Nancy, because my partner was there, always with me. I've waited 20 years for this moment to arrive—to have my wife by my side again, to be called "Tim and Nancy" again. Like her name is mine and mine is hers, and we are truly acknowledging our oneness.

I've spent ten years climbing out of a pit of where it was all just about me, working my way back to Nancy, to myself, to my faith and trust in the Lord. God schooled me on the potter's wheel. He's reshaped and rehabbed me to perfection. I was a house rehabber, now rehabbed by the Lord. Real estate was my business, but I am like the shell of a house now for God to mold and renew, improve and beautify. God is my CEO.

Philippians 1:6

> *⁶ being confident of this, that he who began a good work in you will carry it on to completion until the day of Christ Jesus.*

I'm being sanctified for this purpose of touching others. He has a greater moment for me than I've yet known or could ever imagine just in my mind. I get His help and am His helper to build in the Kingdom with a plan of salvation. One person at a time.

He asks me, "Do you hear My call? Can you step up to the plate? Will you answer My call?"

God is looking for people to answer the call. He's asking for people to humble themselves, to surrender themselves, to give themselves 100% to Him, to let go of the push-pull of the world we are living in and go within to the easy Guidance that is out there.

I've answered the call. I'm excited about the journey that Nancy and I are to embark upon.

Most of all, I'm excited to have my teammate back, to have Nancy by my side, to be by her side—stronger together than we've ever been before, a mission greater than we could ever imagine.

Scared to death, but ready to run the race. Amen.

CHAPTER ELEVEN

———

Nancy Speaks Again

Tim's first confession totally broke me. I lacked the strength to persevere alone. I could not get enough of reading the Bible. God spoke to me daily. I had never felt so close to Him.

During this time, I poured myself into the Bible. One counselor told me to start in Psalms, so every day I would read a psalm in the Book of Psalms. I read a daily devotional, and I read Power of a Praying Wife daily.

God put good Christian friends around to support me, but my best friend was Jesus, and my best guidance was His Word. I talked to Christian women for help. Our pastor and his family were lifesavers for us; we talked to them all the time. They were available day or night to come over when we were having trouble. They were such a blessing to our family. God used them in a mighty way to help us.

My Change

I owe God my life; I owe Him my family, my children, my all. God can do the impossible.

God showed me His great love for me when I was feeling very unlovable. God's love is so much greater than any human love. God let me feel it for a moment one day, and it was simply amazing.

I am very different because of this whole experience. I would not want to go through it again, but I would say that I was "refined" through the fire. God is not done with me.

I love to help women, even more so now, who are going through the same experience that I have. We love to help couples whose marriages are in trouble. We feel the need to use our trials to reach out and help others get through the same type of situation.

Mark 10:27

> *Jesus looked at them and said, "With man this is impossible, but not with God."*

All things are possible with God. God can work through the impossible situations in our life. He says, "Trust me. Give them to me."

1 Samuel 17:47

> *"Remember," He says, "The battle is the Lord's."*

He also says in Philippians 4:13

> *"I can do all things through Christ who gives me strength."*

Tim's Change

God has greatly changed my husband.

After several years, God called him to be a preacher. Yes, a preacher! When he finally humbled himself and confessed his sins, he was a broken and empty vessel. Now God says, "I can use you." He told Tim, "Preach and teach to my people."

What a wonderful transformation it was! From a caterpillar to a butterfly. My husband was preaching and telling the good news to the people. It was great.

Tim also became a much better father. He is home much more. He was able to go to all the girls' sporting events. He drove them to school. He has been there so much more. He has become the real head of the household again. He has been leading, training, and instructing his children in the way to live. He is a very good father.

Life is not always easy for us. There are still ups and downs, and there are still some slips and falls. It's much less; things are much better. We have learned to trust God in all our circumstances. I hope this book will encourage you to do the same. God Bless.

My favorite verse that I want to end with is Jeremiah 29:11–13

11 "For I know the plans I have for you," declares the LORD, "plans to prosper you and not to harm you, plans to give you hope and a future.

12 Then you will call on me and come and pray to me, and I will listen to you.

13 You will seek me and find me when you seek me with all your heart."

CHAPTER TWELVE

——

Final Thoughts

I believe I need to add this chapter to the book as a summary of the revelation that God has given me through this process of surrendering and rehabbing myself.

Living Free

The question is, "How do you live free?"

How do you walk in freedom? How does a Christian become free? We know it's through the salvation of following Jesus, adhering to His Teaching and His Word.

What is free? Sin is broken off from Christians like an elephant that was chained and not understanding that it is released. It's the open prison cell that you refuse to leave. What does it mean that a Christian will sin no more? Then why does the Christian proceed to sin?

It's temptation. We have to learn how to follow a new master. There are two sets of rules: There's truth versus the lie. There are feelings versus the new experience. There's the habit versus the new mind. You must read and listen, and then you must decide to act, and act immediately.

There is a temptation to sin, and a choice to follow either the Holy Spirit or Satan's suggestions. Does your body have power over your actions? Or is the memory of your past physical urges and the payoff and the excitement that moves with it that motivate you to succumb to the temptation?

It starts with thought, and that is the spark that gives way to the temptation.

It's a thought that moves through the mental process, and then the mental moves the physical body, and then the action is performed. The repeated action creates the habit, and the habit leads you to death. That is the process and the road that temptation gives us.

How does a Christian stay free? It's the same thought—it is through the right daily actions. It's the repetitive nature that you have to establish. What did Jesus do? If He is our living example, we must model ourselves on Him at all times.

Number one, Jesus spent time with the Father daily. Number two, He did only what the Father told Him to do—nothing of His own will. Number three, only the things that brought glory to his Father did He do. Number four, He served those around Him, and He made their life better as a result of coming in contact with Him. Number five, He was a tool for the power of the Father to flow through.

It brings us to the question "What is truth then?" If we know we must deny the lie, then what is the truth?

In John 18:33–38 we find out, as Jesus tells us, that He is the truth, and everyone who is of the truth can hear His voice being the Word. How did they become part of the truth? Was it not through believing that they become a part of the truth? Until they believe, they are outside of the truth, and cannot hear His words, nor can they understand His words or our words as we share with Him. They must first believe and then enter into the truth and revelation that can be revealed to them through the Word and through their actions and obedience.

Being Set Free

What does it mean to be set free? There are two things that encompass being free.

The first is to be set free from the desire and also from the payoff that sin promises. The payoff is not real. You are not experiencing freedom, but incarceration.

The second revelation is that the mind must determine that it is a lie sent from Satan. Sin is revealed to the Christian. Truth has replaced the lie. You now understand the magic trick. You are no longer amazed at Satan's sleight of hand. The Holy Spirit has made the Christian's soul fearless.

Satan's deception is no longer accepted. The desire dies down. The old man is weak and without strength. The Energizer Bunny is making its final huge kicks. The snake is rolling across itself for the last time. What tasted like Wednesday night's strong lemonade now tastes like colored water. It's a gift from the Holy Spirit, initiated and given long before the individual knows it has been presented. The gift resides within the individual. The Holy Spirit links up with your spirit, and you have power, but it's on reserve. The individual does not initially know how to handle and invoke this power unless it is put to the test and challenged time and time again.

Temptation. Temptation can be likened to the Chinese symbol that means both "danger" and "opportunity." It is not dangerous if we seize the opportunity within. Temptation is not a sin, but an opportunity to overcome. Temptation is an opportunity to grow and use the power that you have within. It is a chance we must seize. It must be recognized by the Christian to decide if he has the heart, desire, words, and actions of Christ. He decides if he submits and obeys the commands expressed in the Word. You now move beyond the normal shame that you feel when you commit the same troubling sin. You know that the prior sin has no hold on you any longer. You now have the power to walk past the temptation. Satan has no game that can conquer you. It will not cause you to fall this time.

The Holy Spirit tipped the scale, and now you're fully sold out to him. This is what 100% looks like. It is that time when you have given Christ everything that is within you. You are now filled with the Holy Spirit. Your every moment focuses on His might. You're led by His desires, and your subconscious and your unconscious decision is to follow Him at all times. You no longer feel naked and ashamed before God. You feel that you can ask God to fill that need and know that He will, and the temptation will pass. You will weather yet another storm, and you will come out on the other side, protected by the wings of your Heavenly Father.

There is no need to ask for the storm to leave our path—just know that we will weather the storm together. The recurrence of storms will always be with us, so will the storm maker and the storm protector. Confidence comes when you know the storm maker and when you know the storm protector, where your private spot is located under His mighty wing. The Christian follower swallows fear and enjoys the peace bestowed upon him. Fear is only false evidence appearing real. Truth now sheds light on this matter. Fear is of Satan. Faith and trust is of God. You must side with faith and trust in the Lord.

God spoke to me Monday night about finishing the book, and this is now the end of the book. This is the final chapter that now must be written.

Free at Last

I am free at last; I am free at last. I can share with others what has taken me 35 years to overcome—my sexual addiction. I am and now have an understanding of how to control and use money as a tool. I no longer chase it as the second challenge that I have. The Lord set me free and gave me power to live as He desires.

He has given you that same spiritual gift as well. I am a new creation—the old has gone, and the new has come. I am an overcomer. Death has lost its sting.

Galatians 2:20

> *"I have been crucified with Christ and I no longer live, but Christ lives in me. The life I now live in the body, I live by faith in the Son of God, who loved me and gave himself for me."*

I am the elephant that for the first time still feels the weight of the chain on my foot but chooses to walk beyond the normal bare spot on the ground. I'm still walking, exploring the newfound world beyond the limits of our mind and the lie that I once believed. God had so much for me, and I have lived so small for so long. I now believe his promise in Jeremiah 29:11.

> *"I have a plan for you," He says, "that will prosper me, and will not harm me."*

I believe that. God is beginning to pour into my life. He is revealing things to me, connecting me with people who have a vision for the Kingdom and a way that we are to respond to his invitation.

I am beginning to amass those people, and I am beginning to live in greater unity with my wife than ever before. Intimacy is blossoming in areas and ways that we have never experienced. We are truly becoming one.

In our new coaching program where we coach individuals together, we just experienced our first coaching retreat, where I had to step out on faith. I had to pay for the retreat out of pocket cash, out of money that had not even been produced yet. I had to walk that path to see what God would reveal. In the week of the retreat, the Lord had two separate incidents that came together, allowing me to pay for the retreat in full.

We're able to send our three children to college for a tuition cost of nearly $100,000 a year, with no way of knowing how we're going to do that on a pastor's and a social worker's salary. Thanks to their various scholarships and grants, it is a lesser amount than that each year. God has allowed us to meet that obligation time and time again.

I don't worry about such things anymore. I don't know how they're going to come about, but that's not for me to worry about, for the Lord tells me in Matthew 6 not to worry about those things. I should focus on the kingdom and gaining His righteousness.

That is what I focus on.

I share with you my trouble, my pain, and my shame, so that as you walk along His path, you will be strengthened and encouraged to know that Jesus Christ our Lord and His Holy Spirit come together to give you the power to do the same. God is not a respecter of individuals. All of us have the equal opportunity to have a relationship with Him and a life that is amazing beyond comprehension if we will surrender our will over to Him and walk the path that He leads us along.

My favorite passage is Proverbs 3:5–6

> [5] *Trust in the LORD with all your heart*
> *and lean not on your own understanding;*
>
> [6] *in all your ways submit to him,*
> *and he will make your paths straight.*

Thank you for taking the time to share in my journey. Now, produce an amazing life through your own journey. It's not just enough to read the questions, but you must read the questions and answer them, and then take part in the activity. That is the action that moves you from standing on the sideline to playing in the game.

CHAPTER THIRTEEN

———

Lessons Learned

Guiding Master Principles I Should've Followed from the Start

By the grace of the Lord, who brought me the ways and means, and who brought the people into my life who believed in me, I was able to learn the following lessons.

Sure, many of them—and not the real estate lessons (those were the easy ones when I finally woke up)—are works in progress. Rather, I am still a work in progress.

I acknowledge that I could have learned these lessons earlier, but the Lord works in mysterious ways, as so many people say, and I accept that learning them in the last four to ten years has been perfect for me.

I must again say to my daughters and wife—I'm sorry it took me so long, but I'm here now. I'm still learning, but I'm here now.

The lessons I learned were about Faith, Family, and Finances. There were a lot a "little lessons," but I think there were some overriding master principles that I had to learn first that before little lessons fell into place.

The First Master Principle was that I must not choose money over God.

The Lord directed me to sell everything. The Lord directed me to live free of debt. I later learned that being free of debt is not just about money, but about relationships with other people (emotional debt) as well.

The Second Master Principle was about security in the world.

Again, the Lord reminded me that He is our provider. Anything we do to provide for ourselves in the world—work, businesses, chasing reputation, or salting away money in retirement accounts—only serves to push away the Lord's providence from us.

The Third Master Principle the Lord brought to me was about facing my double-mindedness and all its risks to my family and myself.

Having to share my transgressions with Nancy and our pastor caused a great shift in my perception of what I had been doing. To teach me this lesson, the Lord had to make sure I got caught red handed. The Lord, however, also brought me tools like fasting and daily Scripture reading to help erase my double-mindedness.

The Fourth Master Principle was about having to share my struggle with sexual sin more publicly.

I shared it with my congregation. I shared it with my children. They say that the teacher learns as much by teaching as the students do. As I led the congregation of my church, I faced Satan, and I listened to the Lord. As I quieted Satan and dropped all that old baggage, I was able to see how the Lord provided spiritually, emotionally and materially for my family and me.

The Fifth Master Principle I learned was that I could and should focus on prioritizing activities and people.

All I had ever focused on before was work and my addictive behaviors. I made a decision to put God first, then Nancy, then my children. My business only came in fourth place and was no longer allowed to spill over into all hours of the day and night. In this way, the Lord showed me how to balance my life. The Lord showed me what was truly important for me.

As a result of that, my Sixth Master Principle allowed me to embrace all the roles of manhood that were available to me.

I finally saw the fullness and richness of relationships that I had been ignoring. Manhood, husbandhood, fatherhood, pastorship. Businessman still came last.

My Seventh Master Principle concerned my life mission.

Till now, I had always thought my mission in life was to make lots of money for a comfortable retirement for my family. Now the Lord was telling me to surrender 100% of my life to Him, and he showed me a way to do that. Our nonprofit organization, Blessings to Others, was one of the ways to surrender to the Lord. Another way was breathing into the lives of people who needed support and assistance. The third way, which I had already undertaken, was to lead a church. Lastly, at least for now, is to coach and speak to other people outside the church proper, and help them live an Amazing Life in the Lord's light.

The Eighth Master Principle, but I am sure it will not be the last, is that by remaining captive to Satan I also enslaved my family and loved ones. I saw that so very late. By freeing myself from that addictive captivity, and reconnecting meaningfully with the Lord, with my wife and my children, my congregation and others in my life, I hope to be a model for their freedom.

Faith, Family and Finances

These are the "little" lessons I learned over four years (from 2004 through 2009).

Finance Lessons

1. Move towards being debt free. Owe nothing but the love for your brothers in Christ.

Too often, my business life was a matter of stealing from Peter to pay Paul. Debt was the rule, not the exception. Debt freedom is about integrity, and I don't mean just money issues. Sinning and hypocritical living from a dual personality—double-mindedness—creates moral debts with those around you and within your spirit and soul. God knows when you lead a secret life, and it is no secret to Him.

2. Money is not my security. God is my security.

In our society, money is the one object that we believe we must secure in order to have all other tangible possessions. "No money, no anything" is what we think. So we chase money as our security in the world. For millennia, the Lord God has been telling us that He is our security. Follow Him and He will provide, but because what He proposes is not initially tangible, we turn away from trust in the Lord God.

3. Do not roll cash from project to project. Each project should profit by itself.

I finally learned this basic business lesson as the best way to get ahead financially. I don't know how long it takes other business people to learn it. Maybe I just missed that class. Each product, each service, each project we offer needs to be its own profit center. I have found that the Lord also guides me on how to do things right so that each project actually does make its own profits.

4. Do not do business with people who talk too much or who must tell you how good they are.

This is really about doing business with people who listen to God's guidance. If they listen to God's guidance, they won't talk too much. They present themselves humbly to you. They don't need to take credit. I learned to be that person myself—one who doesn't go off on a talking jag or brag about "me, me, me." Remembering that I am a tool—God is doing His work through me, so what do I have to brag about then? I didn't "do" anything; I was the tool. It's a hard row to hoe, but we can do it if we just get quiet and listen to Guidance from Above.

5. Do not let tenants move into the unit until 100% of the security deposit is collected.

This harkens back to every project, product, or service needing to be its own profit center. I rented apartments for a living. I needed to treat it like a business and do so by following processes and procedures that I would never deviate from.

6. File for eviction the first moment you suspect rent will not be paid.

You must let the tenant understand you will not be taken advantage of. Charity is one thing. Business is another. Protect your family. Collect the rent.

7. Always prospect for buyers and good people.

Go out looking for good buyers and do it continuously. Help yourself first. This demonstrates your intention to Him, and He acts for you and through you. The Lord will be there to help you … and bring the right people to you at the right time.

8. Provide for your family. Put them first in the pay column.

I thought that I had been providing for my family first, that I had been putting them first in the pay column, but that ended up being incorrect thinking. Paying my family wasn't a matter of money I was chasing after, it was a matter of love. Provide materially for your family, oh yes. Provide them with an abundance of love first, however, and everything will fall into place. I recently read a book that said that out of the first $250,000, pay yourself 50% for salary, 5% for profit, 10% for taxes, and the remaining 35% is for operating capital.

Family Lessons

9. Slow down your life and take time to enjoy life and family.

We all act like we're in a life-or-death rat race. This comes from an old Protestant work ethic, but there is more to it than that. I was guilty of this when I flailed around trying to be a millionaire and build material security for my family and retirement. I was like this when I pretended I had no time for Nancy or our beautiful children (but had time for my addictions). When God is in your life, and you make time daily to meet with Him, He will make time for your loved ones a conscious priority on your part. The Lord creates the time for you to be with them.

10. Order of life: God, Spouse, Children, Work. Then others.

As I discovered—perhaps far too late in regards to my children, and may all three forgive me—we do have time for that which is important to us. The trick is to unearth our real top priority. As I said above, money is no security to mortal man, but God is. It all starts with God. That means following God must be our priority. God is Love and Compassion. God is Right Guidance. That means the love of people closest to us in our lives must be a consistent priority. When I stopped making exceptions to these rules, I started walking a straight path of Love.

11. Be the priest of the home. Servant leader.

Understand that God has established an order to the family. He has established the husband as the head. He is responsible for working with his wife in unity, but remains ultimately responsible for the outcomes and actions of his family. Lead, lead, lead!

12. Your spouse is not your enemy.

Look into her eyes and say this, "My wife is not my enemy." Stand back to back with your spouse. While you stand back to back, you will detect the real enemy coming your way and will be able together to defeat this adversary.

13. Make a list of the best qualities of your spouse.

List the qualities you notice today (for yourself also). Post the list in a place you can refer to often. Notice how the list evolves as you add to it tomorrow and the next day.

14. Honor you spouse above your children by taking time out to date your mate.

Let the little ones see you prioritizing your spouse. They'll have their time with you. Prioritize the important one—God—first, then spouse, then children.

15. Take your spouse out on a date a least twice per month, no excuses. Weekly is better!

16. Weekends are for family. Sundays are for God. No work on Sundays. Sit and rest, reflect on God's goodness. Take a nap. Slow down.

17. Walk in agreement with your spouse. Discuss all major decisions with your spouse in the presence of the Lord by prayer and conversation.

18. Pray before all serious conversations or during heated conversations.

Prayer is the Christians' approach for quieting the reactive mind and the tense body. Prayer is the Christians' approach for requesting divine guidance and receiving it. Prayer is an approach that can stop arguments cold as you and the other agree to "go to your corners" for five minutes of individual quiet prayer. Prayer calms the heat. Prayer dissolves the stubbornness so we can listen and hear the other person. Prayer can return us to our quiet, calmer self. In business or private life, pray.

19. One willing committed party in a relationship is enough to get started with.

The other person is not the problem. You start with one willing individual to heal the family. Controlling a relationship can never, ever mean that you force the other to change, because they just won't. All you do is make them resist you and your wishes. Controlling a relationship can only ever mean that you are willing and able to change yourself from within. When I willingly started to change myself, I saw real shifts in my relationship with Nancy and with others. Now I realize that if something is not going well, I need to look within me and change my thinking.

20. Always keep the children informed in the marriage relationship. They will know something is wrong, anyway.

Any human relationship, and a marriage relationship is no different, has an energy. Your children are most definitely in tune with that energy. I have discovered that they are often in tune with the energy as a matter of mere survival, if only in a subconscious manner for them. In other words, verbalizing the nature of what's going on in your relationship will only consciously confirm what they have been feeling subconsciously in the first place. Never underestimate a child's understanding of what is going on in his or her environment. If you are hypocritical or hiding something, they will know it. If there is anger and resentment in the house, they will know it. It is best to come clean as soon as you have achieved clarity yourself. If not, they may think it is something they did and in the end blame themselves, and this is never anything you want to plant in your child.

21. Be obedient to God always. Do His will first.

We prioritize God, faith, and our spiritual growth by looking towards the Lord's love and guidance. We get quiet so that we can hear His voice and His will clearly, without any interference from our ego, from the world that is tempting us and distracting us, from our pride, from the noise of our arrogant human selves.

22. Surrender to the Lord in all areas of your life.

Remember—surrender. Listening to God and following His will before your own is not just for Sunday church meetings. It is not just for the management of your relationships. It is not just guidance for how you should work in the world. It is all of these, and everything else that you deal with or face in your life. The Lord is your number one mentor, your number one guide, your number one source of truth. The Lord God is your source of answers to all questions.

23. You have to forgive to live. If you don't forgive, you won't be forgiven. Forgiveness is about setting yourself free and not about the other person.

24. In any given relationship, both people bring good and bad luggage.

There is no perfect individual coming into your relationship. People have a history, like you do. They bring their family history and their experience of it into your relationship. How often have I come back to being judgmental? We only know that another's baggage is good or bad from our perception and judgment of it, and when we stop being judgmental, we can accept the other person simply for who and what he is … now … today.

25. The Bible is the spoken word of God and is useful in all situations. Start there.

It has been my blessed experience to find answers in the Bible when I have a specific question or seek Divine Guidance. Now? I start there. Now that I am open to the Lord speaking through the pages of the Bible, I heed the messages much more readily. No matter what the situation or circumstance.

26. Book of Love: The Song of Solomon.

Read aloud to your spouse. Look at her and mean it. Understand the feeling created within you when you mean it and when she is listening.

Faith Lessons

27. Never speak for the other person or try to determine their motive for what they are doing. You need to use "I" statements when expressing yourself or your feelings in a heated conversation.

28. Never judge the apology of another. Just determine whether or not you will accept it at that time. Forgiveness sets you free.

29. Insanity is doing the same thing over and over and expecting different results.

30. Feelings cannot always be trusted. Love is a commitment, not a feeling. It is work. Daily effort.

31. Never make your Lord the same size or smaller than your problems. God is larger than we could ever imagine.

32. When I need to draw myself back to the compassion and love that Jesus exhorted us to display, I go back to

1 Corinthians 13: 4–8:

> [4] *Love is patient, love is kind. It does not envy, it does not boast, it is not proud.*
>
> [5] *It does not dishonor others, it is not self-seeking, it is not easily angered, it keeps no record of wrongs.*
>
> [6] *Love does not delight in evil but rejoices with the truth.*
>
> [7] *It always protects, always trusts, always hopes, always perseveres.*
>
> [8] *Love never fails. But where there are prophecies, they will cease; where there are tongues, they will be stilled; where there is knowledge, it will pass away.*

Bible Verses that Have Helped Me on My Journey

I have spent countless hours in the Word. Here, in addition to scripture I cite throughout the book, is some scripture that helped me in profound ways as I rehabbed my life with the Lord.

James 5:16

> *Confess your sins to each other and pray for each other, so that you may be healed.*

Philippians 1:6

> *And I am certain that God, who began the good work within you, will continue his work until it is finally finished on the day when Christ Jesus returns.*

Proverbs 3:5–6

> *[5] Trust in the Lord with all your heart and lean not on your own understanding;*
>
> *[6] in all your ways submit to him, and he will make your paths straight.*

Matthew 6:33–34

> *[33] But seek first his kingdom and his righteousness, and all these things will be given to you as well.*
>
> *[34] Therefore do not worry about tomorrow, for tomorrow will worry about itself. Each day has enough trouble of its own.*

Joshua 22:5

> *But be very careful to keep the commandment and the law that Moses the servant of the Lord gave you: to love the Lord your God, to walk in obedience to him, to keep his commands, to hold fast to him and to serve him with all your heart and with all your soul.*

Ephesians 4:1

⁴ As a prisoner for the Lord, then, I urge you to live a life worthy of the calling you have received.

Matthew 16:19

¹⁹ I will give you the keys of the kingdom of heaven; whatever you bind on earth will be bound in heaven, and whatever you loose on earth will be loosed in heaven.

Psalm 66:16–20

¹⁶ Come and hear, all you who fear God; let me tell you what he has done for me.

¹⁷ I cried out to him with my mouth; his praise was on my tongue.

¹⁸ If I had cherished sin in my heart, the Lord would not have listened;

¹⁹ but God has surely listened and has heard my prayer.

²⁰ Praise be to God, who has not rejected my prayer or withheld his love from me!

Psalm 51:4

Against you, you only, have I sinned and done what is evil in your sight; so you are right in your verdict and justified when you judge.

Romans 8:28

And we know that in all things God works for the good of those who love him, who have been called according to his purpose.

1 Peter 5:2

Be shepherds of God's flock that is under your care, watching over them—not because you must, but because you are willing, as God wants you to be; not pursuing dishonest gain, but eager to serve.

Deuteronomy 5:33

Walk in obedience to all that the Lord your God has commanded you, so that you may live and prosper and prolong your days in the land that you will possess.

Hebrews 11:6

And without faith it is impossible to please God, because anyone who comes to him must believe that he exists and that he rewards those who earnestly seek him.

1 Peter 5:6-7

6 Humble yourselves, therefore, under God's mighty hand, that he may lift you up in due time.

7 Cast all your anxiety on him because he cares for you.

Romans 12:1-2

1 Therefore, I urge you, brothers and sisters, in view of God's mercy, to offer your bodies as a living sacrifice, holy and pleasing to God—this is your true and proper worship.

2 Do not conform to the pattern of this world, but be transformed by the renewing of your mind. Then you will be able to test and approve what God's will is—his good, pleasing and perfect will.

Galatians 5:16

16 So I say, walk by the Spirit, and you will not gratify the desires of the flesh.

Psalm 139:23-24

23 Search me, God, and know my heart; test me and know my anxious thoughts.

24 See if there is any offensive way in me, and lead me in the way everlasting.

Psalm 19:14

May these words of my mouth and this meditation of my heart be pleasing in your sight, LORD, my Rock and my Redeemer.

Philippians 4:8

Finally, brothers and sisters, whatever is true, whatever is noble, whatever is right, whatever is pure, whatever is lovely, whatever is admirable—if anything is excellent or praiseworthy—think about such things.

Romans 6:12-14

12 Therefore do not let sin reign in your mortal body so that you obey its evil desires.

13 Do not offer any part of yourself to sin as an instrument of wickedness, but rather offer yourselves to God as those who have been brought from death to life; and offer every part of yourself to him as an instrument of righteousness.

14 For sin shall no longer be your master, because you are not under the law, but under grace.

Deuteronomy 8:18

> *But remember the LORD your God, for it is he who gives you the ability to produce wealth, and so confirms his covenant, which he swore to your ancestors, as it is today.*

The Bibliography of My Rehab

Alongside the Bible, which is ever present and always has first place, here are some of the many books that have influenced me over the past decade of rehabbing who and what I am.

My pastor brought some, and Nancy or my kids brought others. The rest were recommended during seminars we attended. All of them have helped me grow in one or more ways.

They have helped bring me closer to the Lord and an understanding of His Guidance through His Word. Listening to the Lord has brought me closer to my daughters and my wife. Listening to the Lord has brought me to the work I am to do for Him in this life.

Yes, in some way, each of the following books was instrumental in carving out the path that I still follow.

Books That Shaped My Life during My Rehab Process

1. *The Holy Bible*: New International Version; New Living Translation
2. *The Power of a Praying Husband,* Stormie Omartian
3. Family Life Weekend to Remember; The Art of Marriage (Nancy and my first couples weekend in Chicago in 2004)
4. *His Needs, Her Needs: Building an Affair-Proof Marriage,* Willard F. Harley, Jr.

5. *The Five Love Languages,* Gary Chapman
6. *WordSpeak: His Word, Your Voice,* Laura C. Bower
7. *Praying for the Impossible,* Buddy Harrison
8. *Fasting Journal,* Jentezen Franklin
9. *Every Man's Battle: Winning the War on Sexual Temptations One Victory at a Time,* Fred Stoeker and Stephen Arterburn
10. *Strengthen Your Marriage,* Wayne A. Mack
11. *Mighty Men: The Starter's Guide to Leading Your Family,* John Crotts
12. *Victory over the Darkness: Realize the Power of Your Identity in Christ; The Bondage Breaker,* Neil T. Anderson
13. *LIFEONAIRE,* Steve Cook, Shaun McCloskey
14. *Exquisite Agony: Healing for Christians Who Have Been Hurt By Other Christians,* Gene Edwards
15. *E-Myth,* Michael Gerber
16. *The 5 Sex Needs of Men and Women,* Dr. Gary and Barbara Rosberg
17. *Do Yourself a Favor, Love Your Wife,* Dr. H. Page Williams
18. *Total Forgiveness,* R.T. Kendall
19. *The Circle Maker: Praying Circles around your Biggest Dreams and Greatest Fears,* Mark Batterson
20. *Seeking the Face of God,* Gary L. Thomas
21. *Holiness for Ordinary People,* Keith Drury
22. *Dating my Daughter; Interviewing Your Daughter's Date: 8 Steps to No Regrets,* Dennis Rainey
23. *Getting to Know the Holy Spirit,* Mahesh and Bonnie Chavda
24. *Prayer,* O. Hallesby
25. *Transformed into His Likeness,* Armand P. Tiffe
26. *Closing the Window: Steps to Living Porn Free,* Tim Chester
27. *Fixing the Money Thing,* Gary Keesee
28. *Experiencing God, Knowing and Doing the Will of God,* Henry and Richard Blackaby and Claude King

How to Reach Tim Grimmett

The author, Tim Grimmett, is available for a limited number of speaking engagements, corporate and Christian workshops, and group and private coaching assignments. He also has a selection of training programs and mentoring programs. For information, contact Tim Grimmett at:

Amazing Life - Now
2166 North Waterford Drive
St. Louis, MO 63033

tim@TimGrimmett.com

Free Resources

Webinar: Amazing Life Mindset, Get It Now!!!
Basic Amazing Life Plan Worksheets
    www.AmazingLife-Now.com/Plan
Passive Income Plan
    www.hafpinc.com/passiveincome

Your Next Move: Action, Action, Action

Download the 10 Day Challenge – First Step to a New Life
    www.AmazingLife-Now.com/10daychallenge

www.ingramcontent.com/pod-product-compliance
Lightning Source LLC
LaVergne TN
LVHW051244080426
835513LV00016B/1730